Praise

"He turns a perceptive eye on the black experience in contemporary America, from the virulent hatred of a David Duke to black-on-black racism. The book certainly will provoke controversy."
— *Publishers Weekly*

"Wiley writes with a zinging, lifting, angry, cutting honesty that makes you sit up and pay attention. He writes so deftly that he keeps the reader entranced. It's an important book."
— Robert Creamer, author of *Babe: The Legend Comes To Life*

"Must reading for anyone who thinks, feels, and wants to stretch intellectually."
— John R. Thompson, Jr., Georgetown University

"Wiley's thought-provoking work is filled with amusing anecdotes and controversial commentaries that may help to dispel many misconceptions."
— *Library Journal*

"Wiley aims his considerable wit and literary style at larger issues. . . . Provocative ideas from a sharp writer."
— Nelson George, author of *The Death of Rhythm & Blues*

"Wiley shows a folksy, homespun brilliance."
— *San Francisco Examiner & Chronicle*

"I think it is funny, angry, passionate, rational. . . . It's a book that sort of sneaks up on you, jabs you, dances away, then levels you."
— Dick Schaap, ABC News

"Wiley skillfully marshalls his anger into prose that achieves power through understatement. . . . A bold new voice."
— *The Los Angeles Times Book Review*

PENGUIN BOOKS

WHY BLACK PEOPLE TEND TO SHOUT

Ralph Wiley is an author, journalist, and writer who has worked for the Knoxville, Tennessee *Spectrum*, *The Oakland Tribune*, and, for nine years, *Sports Illustrated*, as a staff writer, senior editor, and special contributor. He also has written articles for *Premiere*, *Emerge*, and *Sportsview* magazines, the pilot for the TV series *The Other Side of Victory*, and has appeared as a commentator on NBC, ESPN, BET, and CNN. In 1987, he formed Heygood Images Productions, Inc., a multimedia concept and consulting firm. His first book, *Serenity: A Boxing Memoir*, was published in 1988. He is currently at work on a collection of stories, and is the co-author of John Thompson's forthcoming autobiography. Mr. Wiley lives outside Washington, D.C.

WHY BLACK PEOPLE TEND TO SHOUT

Cold Facts and Wry Views From a Black Man's World

Ralph Wiley

PENGUIN BOOKS

To the Sphinx,
and Dorothy
and Ralph

PENGUIN BOOKS
Published by the Penguin Group
Viking Penguin, a division of Penguin Books USA Inc.,
375 Hudson Street, New York, New York 10014, U.S.A.
Penguin Books Ltd, 27 Wrights Lane,
London W8 5TZ, England
Penguin Books Australia Ltd, Ringwood,
Victoria, Australia
Penguin Books Canada Ltd, 10 Alcorn Avenue, Suite 300,
Toronto, Ontario, Canada M4V 3B2
Penguin Books (N.Z.) Ltd, 182–190 Wairau Road,
Auckland 10, New Zealand

Penguin Books Ltd, Registered Offices:
Harmondsworth, Middlesex, England

First published in the United States of America by
Carol Publishing Group 1991
Published in Penguin Books 1992

1 3 5 7 9 10 8 6 4 2

"On the Natural Superiority of Black Athletes" appeared in *Emerge* magazine, vol. 1,
no. 2, October 1989.
"Witness for the Prosecution" appeared in *Emerge* magazine, vol. 1, no. 3, January 1990.

THE LIBRARY OF CONGRESS HAS CATALOGUED THE HARDCOVER AS FOLLOWS:
Wiley, Ralph.
Why black people tend to shout : cold facts and wry views from a
black man's world / Ralph Wiley.
p.   cm.
"A Birch Lane Press book."
ISBN 1-55972-073-5 (hc.)
ISBN 0 14 01.6853 2 (pbk.)
1. Afro-Americans—Social life and customs.   I. Title.
E185.86.W45   1991
305.896'073—dc20   90–28665

Printed in the United States of America

Contents

About Travel

About Life

Why Black People Tend to Shout

Why do black people tend to shout? Now there is a question for the ages. Black people tend to shout in churches, movie theaters, and anywhere else they feel the need to shout, because when joy, pain, anger, confusion and frustration, ego and thought, mix it up, the way they do inside black people, the uproar is too big to hold inside. The feeling must be aired.

First of all, black people are too happy just being able to shout not to take advantage of the luxury. When you have read that bits were put in some of your ancestors' mouths, you tend to shout. When a sweet grandmotherly sort has to tell you how black people once were chained in iron masks in the canebrake, to keep them from eating the cane while they harvested it, and that these masks were like little ovens that cooked the skin off their faces—when you hear that grandmotherly voice and realize she once was a girl who might have been your girl, and someone caused this pain on her lips and nobody did anything about it but keep living—this gives you a tendency to shout, especially when confronted by an opportunity to speak to a smarmy talk-show host or a snarling highway patrolman.

Black people are too smart not to shout, especially when happiness comes in for a short visit before it has to go on down the road. We want happiness to know it's appreciated when it comes calling. Poverty has something to do with the shouting, too. Most black people can't afford to be quiet.

Black people shout because they want the answers to questions that go unasked. Like, who knocked the nose and lips off the Sphinx?

Black people tend to shout because they appreciate these and all of life's other good jokes which started off as tragedies. We have to. The Bert Williamses, Pryors, Murphys and Cosbys didn't become funny by accident. Life gave them material. Laugh or die.

Black people tend to shout because nothing has come close to making those of the African diaspora less determined, or less artistic, or less inventive, or less adaptable, or less productive, or less wise, or less creative, or less quite stupendously gorgeous.

Black people shout because they are immortal and sense this. Black people sense this because we have been dying for years, shouting and dying, yet here black people are, the salt of the earth. Here we are.

Black people tend to shout because nothing can stop a new meaning in life with each passing generation.

Black people tend to shout because they dare to have the nerve to not be silent.

If black people didn't shout, who would? Now *there* is a question for the ages.

Work and Business

How Black People Work Under Pressure

I paused one evening when I was living in New York City. This was news in itself, for I rarely paused while I was living in New York. I never had time for that. I even ran to the bathroom. Everything I did had to be done right away, stat, ASAP, now, yesterday, and what's more, it all had to be done by law. I hardly had the chance to notice where I was living.

I believe it was on the corner of 106th Street and Manhattan Avenue. As I shot past one day, it occurred to me that the crack cocaine dealerships in the neighborhood outnumbered the newsstands three to one. But I had grown up in a house that stood within a block of six liquor stores, and I hadn't noticed that until much later.

I had no time to notice in New York either, because I was too busy working. I had to keep going, keep pushing, keep moving, because I had to survive. That meant I had to get things done *now*. My back was to the wall in New York, and I was too busy to pause for the likes of the "NBC Nightly News" with Tom Brokaw.

One evening, Brokaw wound up his show with what is called "a heartwarming human interest piece." I have

developed dependable antennae for what is usable, sal-
vageable, what can be modified to provide succor or
sustenance in my quest to live. I know instinctively,
without thinking, what to keep and what to throw away.
I felt my invisible antennae vibrate, so I took a chance. I
slowed down and took note.

It seems two little girls were walking along a frozen
river somewhere on the American-Canadian border—on
which side, I don't recall. It wasn't essential. The girls
were talking, probably discussing little-girlisms and sharing their best little-girl secrets. They might have been ten
years old. Probably younger, as I remember. One of the
girls was white and one was black and that didn't matter
either, not until they got a little too adventurous and
wound up slipping through the ice and into the frozen
river.

Up on a nearby hillside, three white men were doing
some amateur filming with a hand-held remote video
camera and minding their own business in general when
one of them looked down and saw the little girls in the
frozen river. Another man filmed the entire exercise from
there. We saw the view from the hillside and then the
"NBC Nightly News" made the cut to the frozen river,
where one of the men was engaged in the classic ice-
saving technique, stretched out flat to spread his weight
near the safe shore, reaching out with a long but flimsy
stick for the little black girl, while his ankles were secured
by one of his friends.

The other recorded the events for posterity. The stick
was extended toward the girl as she began to tire even
more. Only her face and neck and one arm remained
above the water. She had to be chilled to her very mar-
row by now.

It was difficult to tell how long she had been immersed
in the icy river, due to the cutting and editing of the tape.
This much was certain. The little white girl was already
out of the water and was probably bundled up in

something warm. We had not seen the rigors of her rescue. The men might have saved her, then discussed the dangers of walking on thin ice with the little white girl for a while before they turned their attention to the little black girl. As I say, we'll never know, because the video-tape was edited.

The tape rolled on without narration. We could see the man extending the stick. We could hear him yelling, telling the little black girl to grab the stick if she wanted to live. Expletives were bleeped from the tape. The rescuer was cursing in his frustration with the girl because she wasn't showing quite enough initiative, telling her "Bleep-bleep, yes, you can!" Almost like it was undoubtedly her fault that the girls had tumbled into the river in the first place.

Apparently all this was a great and quick lesson in life for the little black girl, for she willed motor function and life into her frozen limbs and pulled herself out of the jagged hole in the ice and away from a certain and untimely death. Then the three men gave the two little girls a ride home and all of them were glad no one had died.

One little girl had been rescued. One little girl had survived. The men were heroes. But the little black girl was more heroic and would have to be from now on. This was a secret she wouldn't be able to share with the other little girl. Now she had to live with her own special secret.

Tom Brokaw came back on and smiled a bit at this heartwarming story. I signed off before he did. I had to go.

Hair

Around Christmastime in 1987, Pamela Mitchell, an employee of a Marriott hotel in Washington, D.C., received an ultimatum for the J. W. Marriott Corporation. Pamela was dutifully informed that her services as a reservationist would no longer be required unless she did something with her hair. Pamela wore her hair woven in exquisitely neat braids, *sans* extensions, with a bang flip. This seemed sweet to me but was unacceptable at the Marriott. Or was it that Pamela's blackness, her thick, tightly curling black hair, was unacceptable at Marriott? Bo Derek tried to wear her hair like that and white people called her a "10." And Bo Derek probably couldn't take a reservation to save her life.

Now, black people will let white people tell them many things, and usually be convinced the white people are right. But when it comes to hair, well, you can't tell black people anything. We each have our own ideas. It would be like telling white people about tanning in the sun, or Orientals about face powder, or Mediterraneans about blond dye.

The hair trip is an endless ongoing curling circling mass of black people who have been straightening, frying, processing, conking, waving, texturizing, cutting, shaving, parting, hot-ironing, cold-waving, stocking-capping, Jheri-curling, activating, reactivating, oiling, braiding, Afrotiquing, natty dreading, Quo Vadising and otherwise fiddling with their hair for years. A great beauty is constructed and a great profit piled up in all this activity. The Marriott Corporation told Pamela her hair didn't present a "good business image." This seemed unduly naïve on Marriott's part. Usually, the successful corporation can smell business a mile away, like a shark senses bloody water.

One widespread theory on the reason God gave black people our hair in the first place is that God always wanted us to have some business of our very own. God is all-knowing. God must have foreseen that black people would have less than a head start in the world trade market such as it is currently constructed. So, in another moment of brilliance, God was God. And black hair was black hair.

Uniqueness can be seen as aberrant. Beauty is in the eyes of the beholder, to muster the proper cliché. Black people had suffered so much racism, so many humiliations, including a procedure in Louisiana called "the hair test," that we began to wonder if, hey, maybe it's the hair that drives white people off the deep end. They're always flipping theirs around. Maybe it's a fetish. Can't rule it out.

This idea came into people's heads as a result of a lack of global mass communication. If the black people who had this notion had been able to speak with their dark-skinned cousins in Australia—an enviable, nomadic tribe who came to be called aboriginals (the very meaning of which is an insult)—they would have had to change their minds about the source of white people's bad attitudes about putting up with this "different style."

For the aboriginals had some hair on them. There was nothing bad about that. They had the curls, like the African people, only much looser, and they had the relative straightness and the looseness of European hair, only much thicker. Their hair had a texture and meaning like few others on earth and was usually a rich, uniform shade of blue-blackness.

The aboriginals wore this hair like earthly halos, according to the stained glass. This hair style did not change any opinions regarding their place in Australia. The people who were harmless and had the "good" hair were still treated as abnormal, abstract, abstruse, absurd and, in all probability, much, much too abundant.

But due to lack of knowledge about this, and from receiving many other signals, people of African descent here in America took a cue from more nearby sources and called their hair "bad" and "nappy." Eventually hair had different, unofficial but quite relevant "grades," going all the way over to so-called absolutely straight hair, which, I've been told, is usually the province of the Oriental and Mongoloid peoples, and less so of the European-based stock. If you think about it, you can also find straight hair on your average orangutan or polar bear, but some-how—and you can check someone in marketing on this—straight hair ended up being called "good hair," and even "Nearer My God to Thee" hair. And, sure enough, if you went to the nearest church, temple or cathedral, usually there was the straight-haired Jesus in the stained glass, looking up beatifically, not needing so much as a single shot of Sta-Sof-Fro.

Black hair care has become a one-billion-dollar-a-year business, thanks to the ideas of Madame C. J. Walker. Maybe Marriott wasn't so naïve after all. Maybe their honchos had been noshing with Revlon's. That corporate giant had seen its chief, one Irving Bottner, proclaim earlier in 1987 that the largest part of this billion would soon be taken over by the likes of Revlon, leaving the black-owned hair care companies, like Soft Sheen, Johnson, M&M, World of Curls, Luster's, D-orum and Bronner Brothers in the dust. Bottner said their products were inferior. But of course, he would say that. It was good business for him to say that.

Now, black people have been making small, large and larger fortunes off our own hair for years. You already know this if your last name is Gardner or Johnson and you live in Chicago, or if you live in Indianapolis and are by any chance a direct descendant of Madame C. J. Walker. The black-owned companies rose up in arms about the arrogance and good public relations of Revlon. White people have borrowed many things from black people over the years, but black people never thought they'd be coming for our hair.

I have relatives in the black hair care business. They live much better than I do. They're working and working steady. When they see a head of virgin black hair, the light comes on in their eyes and they smile. "Why don't you let me do something with that?" they say ever so sweetly. Then they proceed to do whatever it is, and all for just a nominal fee. Then your hair grows out or back and you can see the genius of this business. The market will always be there.

The people who traditionally had the biggest smiles in the black community were invariably the barbers, the beauticians, the beauty supply wholesalers and retailers, and the morticians. Currently, the barbers are back with an unholy vengeance, doing bustling business due to black hair. The new wave is hair sculpture, or, in other words, the barber's revenge for the sixties and early seventies, when busy barbershops were as rare as busy wax museums. A few people went to look around. I missed going to the barbershops and am glad to see the trend as it is today.

A few years ago, a woman who was supposed to be my companion came home crying, and I, ever the fool, asked her why. She said she had stared at a man's head of hair while she was at a nearby shopping mall. She said she couldn't help staring at the man's thick, curly hair. I said,

"Well, that sounds reasonable enough to me," and kept reading the newspaper. She kept repeating, "But don't you understand?"

This seemed strange to me until a few weeks later when I decided she was talking about me. My hair apparently was not thick and curly enough to make her weep. I had never even considered that my hair would provoke any kind of reaction at all. I suppose I had been sheltered. As it turned out, this was not at all unfortunate knowledge. Eventually it helped me to make up my mind to get out of a situation which was not healthy.

Some ten years later, I mentioned to one of my colleagues that I thought the whole Jheri-curl business was ridiculous and anybody who wore one of those treatments was obviously not busy enough at work. I was quite sanctimonious about this until my colleague mentioned that several of our acquaintances suspected I had a Jheri-curl myself. Maybe just a touch-up. But I was putting *something* on my hair, wasn't I? I broke out laughing but stopped quickly when my colleague failed to join me.

Black people definitely put you in check about your hair, one way or another. I was about to complain that I didn't wear a Jheri-curl at all, but then I decided, so what? I had not been immune to the power long given to European tastes in the global mass market. So who was I to judge?

I do not consider any of this poignant now. I have gotten over it by amusing myself. I have attended three or four black hair care "shows," a get-together of stylists, sales and marketing people, chemists, models, pickpockets, all manner of professionals. They were always a stunning sight to behold. Hundreds and sometimes thousands of creative people around, and the least noticeable thing about them all was the way they wore their hair. I was awed by the costumes, the colors, the jewelry, the utter insouciance, by what the French mellifluously call *élan*, and by the come-hither looks from the pretty men and the cold businesslike precision of the handsome women. And the smiles! The teeth! The place hummed like a beehive.

I used to go to the circus when I was a boy, now I watch films, but of all this I prefer the black hair care expositions for reliable entertainment. The black hair care expositions put anything I recall from Ringling Brothers and Barnum & Bailey or MGM to a most absolute shame.

Once I was at one of these shows and a lady asked if she could "do" my hair for me. For *me* she said. As politely as I could, I said my hair had already been done. She asked me, "What do you put on it?" "As little as possible," I said. "Some shampoo, some mineral oil and beeswax potion, a stiff brush and a good comb of a modest length and I'm good to go." She looked at me as if I had suddenly been transformed into an iguana. "Then, may I ask, what are you doing here?" she said in a manner which seemed to suggest I leave.

Marriott suggested the same to Pamela Mitchell, but for different reasons. I saw Pamela's head of hair a little later. Her hair seemed to reflect creativity, superior workmanship, and good judgment on Pamela's part. It revealed that she knew how to make herself a more attractive person—to herself. Since she had to live with the mirror more surely than she had to work in a Marriott, Pamela stuck to her principles, and kept her job *and* her beautiful braids. There really wasn't a question of choosing one over the other. Marriotts and Revlon's products come and go, but black hair is forever. Even if Pamela had lost her job, she could have always moved to Chicago or Indianapolis, opened a hair shop and made a small fortune.

Purple With a Purpose

Alice Walker helped entrench black men at the head of the endangered species list with her book *The Color Purple*. It was a good book nevertheless. Everyone was agreed on that except a few uneasy black men who thought, "Ah, this is just what we needed—something else to hate about ourselves."

Alice Walker was nominated for and awarded a Pulitzer Prize. The Pulitzer Prize is an award thought up by and given out by white men, so it follows the prize would be for the ultimate glorification of their fellows. It is said the award is to reward good or timely writing. Such are the matters which lead to debates.

Alice Walker won a Pulitzer. James Baldwin never won a Pulitzer, even though he could write rings around Alice (and nearly everyone else I've ever read, for that matter). Mr. Baldwin's subject matter was considered too dicey for many people, some of whom apparently were members of the Pulitzer committee. Zora Neale Hurston never won a Pulitzer, even though she could write rings around Alice Walker and even Alice would admit it.

But Ms. Walker had touched a nerve or struck a chord with her masterpiece, and when you are a writer and an artist, this is what you set out to do. So you can't take anything away from Alice Walker. She did her job well. She created art, and art needs no conscience, for it is art. Chinua Achebe, the Nigerian writer, says "All art is propaganda." But only some art is profitable propaganda. Perhaps Alice Walker can now afford a change of heart.

Unlike art, I do have a conscience, I think. And I am not a serious critic of art. I think art is the best way to receive the propaganda you are going to get anyway. However, I reserve the right to criticize Alice Walker. The least I can do is return her favor.

I am a writer. I say I am, at least. In the age of Newspeak I suppose I could be called an alphabet manipulator. I never expect to win the Pulitzer Prize, not because of how I write so much as because of what I write. I like to walk to the edge and look over, and that makes many people who join committees queasy.

Not everyone enjoys flying, or contemplation. I don't always care for it myself unless I am at the controls. And I am not a pilot, so I do my flying elsewhere. This is a bittersweet realization, that my flights will not, have not and do not please all people. We all want to be liked—I learned that by flying with a redheaded white man named Robert Penn Warren—even by the members of the Pulitzer committee. On the other hand . . .

Alice Walker won a Pulitzer for *The Color Purple*, just as Janet Cooke had won one for her story of a fictitious eight-year-old heroin addict in *The Washington Post*. Now *The Color Purple* just happened to contain no black male characters with any redeeming qualities, other than the fact that some of them finally died. The black men in this novel were all roués with crooked teeth, villains of irreducible evil, or insufferable idiots. You can only write well on what you have experienced, so this must have been close to what Alice Walker lived or researched.

The same was true for Janet Cooke. She never met an eight-year-old heroin addict, but she drew from what she did know, horrified it up a bit, made up more for dramatic effect, and the critics loved it so much they insisted it be awarded the Pulitzer Prize. Some black people always thought something was fishy about it.

Unfortunately, Ms. Cooke's story was submitted in the nonfiction category, so they had to take back the Pulitzer Prize when the committee found out she made it all up. Now, Ms. Walker drew from what she knew, horrified it up a little bit, made up some more just for dramatic effect. The critics loved it so much they insisted it be awarded the Pulitzer Prize. Since it had been submitted in the fiction category, Ms. Walker didn't have to give her Pulitzer back. Still, some black men thought there was something fishy about it.

Were the stories linked? Well, there might have been some eight-year-old little black heroin addicts out there somewhere. If Ms. Cooke had only made the young addict ten years older, she probably could have driven around D.C. until she bumped into one. What made the story was its poignance — this little black man, already shot to hell and gone.

The Color Purple was also a poignant story, and one cannot help but admire Ms. Walker's story line, which was inspired. She probably couldn't help but write the book the way she did, for the more shot-to-hell the men were in her story, the more holy the suffering women would be in the end. It was brilliant use of effect.

Ms. Walker had been working on the same technique for years in most of her books, and she finally got just the spin she wanted to put on the ball. The long-suffering women and the abusive men with crooked teeth who beat their own daughters seem to carry a fascination in all of Ms. Walker's work. And as an artist, she is to be applauded for staying busy. The problem here is volume. The reason some black men were uncomfortable was that there was nothing substantive out there to give other impressions about black men. They say any ink is good ink, but black men, above all other ethnic groups in

America with the exception of the Native Ame
know this is not so.

If there were five hundred books by or about black people in any given year and, say, one hundred of them were
good and publicized as such, then *The Color Purple* and
its ilk wouldn't have been seen so narrowly by its critics,
who were largely black and male.

The same goes for the movie *The Color Purple*. Black
people, and especially black men, see themselves in limited and negative roles in film. Aliens, Nazis and black
men from the inner city are the easier villains to identify
at the movies, or such has been my experience there. So
Steven Spielberg was fascinated by Ms. Walker's book and
made a movie out of it. Apparently a work about black
people in America is not considered art unless some stereo-
typical black men are part of it.

I had an editor, a white man, who absolutely loved *The
Color Purple*. I understood that. Editors and I usually
disagree. For an editor, the thing to love about the book
was the story line. Ms. Walker had written much of the
book in what was a broken English version of dialect. I
doubt *The Color Purple* would have gotten the Pulitzer or
been made into a movie by Steven Spielberg just for this
quality. No, the poignant story line was definitely the
clincher.

Time passed, and Toni Morrison, another African-
American woman writer, came out with a book called
Beloved.

The story line in this book was at the least the equal of
that in *The Color Purple*. A mother who murders her own
child rather than leave the child a slave is revisited by
that child later in life. Or is she? In Ms. Morrison's novel,
unlike Ms. Walker's, not all the black men had crooked
teeth and no souls. Ms. Morrison didn't win the National
Book Award, and there was a telling scenario around that
fact. *The Color Purple* had been acclaimed unanimously.

Beloved's status as a work of art was questioned, at least by certain committees and award-givers.

The National Book Award functionaries had Toni Morrison come down to the luxurious Pierre Hotel in New York City for the awards ceremony. There the winner would be announced before the civilized world. People were already congratulating Toni Morrison, and then the announcement came that Mr. Larry Heinemann had won for the novel *Paco's Story*, a book about the homecoming of a Vietnam War veteran. No one applauded this more heartily than Toni Morrison.

The literary critic of *The New York Times*, Michiko Kakutani, wrote a story about this. Apparently, Ms. Kakutani had considered *Beloved* a lock for the National Book Award for fiction. "Members of the literary community had considered Toni Morrison's novel, *Beloved*, a virtual shoo-in." *Beloved* had lost the award two votes to one.

Later, Ms. Kakutani was rebutted in the book review of the *Los Angeles Times*. Jack Miles, the *Times* book editor, leaped to Heinemann's defense. Miles called Ms. Kakutani's story "misleading" and "ungracious." Ms. Kakutani had called *Beloved* "a work of mature imagination—a magisterial and deeply moving meditation not only on the cruelties of a single institution [slavery], but on family, history, and love," and added, "It's unfair perhaps to compare [Heinemann's] second novel with one written by a highly experienced novelist, but then that's exactly what the judges on the fiction panel for the National Book Award did."

To which Miles rebutted: "The judges on the panel compared three novels by relative beginners with one novel by a true veteran, Philip Roth, and one by a novelist, Toni Morrison, who is somewhere in between . . . True, Heinemann has only two novels in print. But then Morrison has only five. There is a clear difference between them, but Kakutani grossly exaggerates it when she speaks of Heinemann as if he were a well-meaning English major and of Morrison as if she were Eudora Welty."

I don't know, but I would think that Toni Morrison would be glad she is who she is and not Eudora Welty. Who knows but that Eudora Welty might owe people money. *Only* five books? How many books made a true veteran? One more than Toni Morrison would ever write, by some tables.

Tucked into Miles's rebuttal of Ms. Kakutani was this nugget: "It is pure accident that Larry Heinemann has written the lead review in today's book review . . . He has written for the book review before. We hope he will write for us again." Somehow, I have no doubt that he will. And since one can review books for the *Los Angeles Times* book review by pure accident, I will immediately go stand on a street corner and wait to be hit by an offer to do so.

Writing is both easy and difficult. It's not as difficult as composing a symphony, but it's not as easy as listening to one. Writing is like falling down. It's not hard, but doing it can hurt. Sometimes you don't land right. It takes nerve and enough ability to make a fairly soft landing to keep trying it. Anybody should be able to write, although few ever end up writing well. All this is strictly a matter of opinion. No one will care what Jack Miles or Michiko Kakutani or I thought about *Beloved* and *Paco's Story* or writing twenty-five years from now. But the books might still be bound, the words still there. And it will be up to the new reader to make the decision on what he or she is moved by.

Awards don't mean anything about the quality or artfulness of a work of writing. In fact, if the critics appreciate a thing when that thing first comes out, that should make it all the more suspect. Great art should be over the head of the critics of its time. That has usually been the case. Critics often miss the boat on art, unless it touches a nerve and strikes a chord, or is useful for propaganda. Being a critic and an award-giver is easy. All you have to do is like something or somebody and make up reasons why or why not. Children do it all the time.

If *Beloved* had featured more male ogres, it would have had a better shot at the National Book Award. Toni Morrison eventually got a Pulitzer Prize for *Beloved*. A group of black writers had petitioned. Of course, this had nothing to do with the decision of the Pulitzer Prize committee, according to the committee, but I don't know.

If there were more black writers, Walker and Morrison could write to their hearts' content and not be concerned about what critics or black men or petitioners think. People aren't damaged if a book or movie about white people offends them. They go down the street to see a different movie, or read a different book. The key is volume. I am trying to keep up my end, but it's a race against time. If Alice Walker has anything to say about it, I only have a few months left before I get my just desserts and the credits roll over my unworthiness and people everywhere rejoice.

The Dark Side of Mencken

The diaries and resulting social debris of the late newspaperman, writer, drinker, teetotaler, stone-heart and victim of lovesickness, H. L. Mencken, were released in 1989. They were met with much consideration and critical review, verging on panic. As I have described him, Mencken, like some people, and nearly all writers, was a galaxy of contradictions. However, he had talent. His talent was said to be for expressing his observations and views through the written word. That he might have been a social cretin on occasion should not hinder the evaluation of his writing in the least. Most writers border on misanthropy, so much so I often wonder why I spent most of my life becoming one.

Mencken's diaries brought ample evidence of his faults and misapprehensions to the surface. Oftentimes he was a bilious malcontent who belittled his friends and their accomplishments behind their backs. He patronized and otherwise rode the backs of people of African ancestry and was ominously silent about Nazism. In fact, he stated that there was but one Jewish man fit to be in his private club in Baltimore, of all places. He spared no one, except perhaps himself.

I am not a Mencken scholar. I am not a scholar of any

sort in the way most mean *scholar* when they use the word. I am a humble scrivener, much as Mencken was. There are only two reasons why I admired him. I was not at all familiar with his writings, only with one single declarative sentence: "No one ever went broke underestimating the intelligence of the American public." In one fell swoop, with this one great line, H. L. Mencken had told the incontrovertible brass truth of things in the simplest manner possible. This is almost the essence of writing. Possibly he came upon this achievement by accident, the way an unskilled, athletic kid could hit one major league pitch on a line into right field with his eyes closed with dumb luck, but would have no chance of hitting major league pitches on a line into right field at a steady average of .300.

Perhaps it was not an accident. Mencken was not a writer of great subtlety, apparently. He never took the time for that—well, at least he didn't in his unvarnished diaries. That is why his version of the essence of writing has to be tempered and taken with pepper. Subtlety is to be admired for its completeness of effect. This was one aspect of his craft—apparently he felt one of the lesser aspects—which Mencken never bothered to master.

That one line, which I read once many years ago and have remembered ever since, was enough for me to admire the writing talent of Mencken. That he also had little use for the historical praise of *Moby-Dick* happens to be another area in which we found agreement.

Mencken may have been racist and anti-Semitic. He was always big on being welcomed into clubs, it seems. I say, as long as he kept it out of people's faces, whatever he did, he did. He won't be able to do much of anything new anymore, so there's no chance he will change his mind. He might not care to change even if he were afforded the opportunity. The only reason there was so much outrage over the contents of his diary was because he was writing for a newspaper. And newspapermen, like many public servants, are presumed to have good characters, most especially including tolerance for their fellow man. I have rarely seen a governor or a football coach or a faith healer about whom it has not been written—at least once—that he was tolerant of his fellow man.

Mencken was obviously thought of in this way—why else the surprise over the contents of his diary? The flaw of his observers is that they believed because Mencken wrote so well, he was well.

He was what he was. Many who were critical of the diary pointed out with great care that living in the time Mencken lived was no excuse for his views. It doesn't justify his crass assumptions and self-aggrandizement, his racism and anti-Semitism, his back-stabbing and lushing. They believe that intelligence is intelligence and should always be able to see things clearly, no matter what.

Some of the very people who wrote these noble comments have themselves uttered the most vile and reprehensible things about their fellow men; have been so drunk they couldn't stand. They can deny it until the cows come home but they won't convince me otherwise. The fact remains that even today, many people, not to mention writers of all races, think in racist or sexist or anti-Semitic or anti-everything tones.

Writers are the greatest narcissists and nihilists this side of painters and dancers. The question is, do they write that way? Do they paint that way? Dance that way? I learned this lesson the hard way through two of the writers whose works I long ago read and admired, Jack London and Richard Wright. I first read a London story, "To Build a Fire," as a freshman in high school. I was an inexperienced child who didn't realize he could appreciate or identify good writing and could not describe it even when he tried. Yet London's skill broke through all of that nonsense and took someone from a different time and another parallel to the time and parallel of London's choosing. He made me feel the cold, in other words. I went on to read many other London stories.

Later, I found out that he had been reared by an African-American matriarch. After he had become an adult and a writer and had begun to have the resulting complex, double-sided, convoluted thoughts—writers live on both sides of the fence if they are true to their writing—he became a vehement racist, as well as a socialist. Any politician can tell you that those two descriptions don't easily go together in the same person. So of course London was or at least seemed to be schizophrenic. It was easier for him to live day to day as an adult and explain certain things away by adopting racism to assuage his own conscience—yet he still needed that egalitarian self for the writing which could reach everyone, including the very people his adult racism vilified and cut short. Indeed, this may have been whom he was trying to reach, lost as he was in his own mind.

London wrote a story called "The Mexican" in which he literally became the oppressed minority figure, battling against the howling tornadoes of racist behavior, innuendo, subtlety and blatant, murderous fact. And within this story, within his protagonist's mind, he dealt with that and overcame it. Simply speaking, London won the fight on paper. London wrote the story. And the same London was an avowed racist in his life beyond the written page.

So should I ever have met Jack London or, by declension, H. L. Mencken on the street—an unlikely proposition at best—and they had said something out of what I considered the realm of good taste, should they have cracked out of turn, well, then they would have had to face me as a man. There would have been a fight and punches would have been thrown and since this is America most likely I would have gone to jail. They not only would *not* have gone to jail but surely would have had their side of the story fairly represented in the press, the cold-hearted, stinking, weak, magnificent bastards.

This is one way writers think. In point of fact, it is impossible for me to meet either man on the street, but should I meet a reasonable facsimile, I would not likely hit him or even speak to him. And if we should fight, the police might not come.

London and Mencken no longer exist except on the page. That they and their flaws no longer exist does not change the power of whatever it is they left on the page. London could have been so racist that either he or I would have had to die, but "The Mexican" is still on the page.

I feel much the same with Mencken, although to a lesser degree. He did have the one great line, and probably more. The one is enough for me.

Richard Wright was another matter. If not for a few years' difference, I suppose I would have been writing in much the same manner. He took me from a lower plane to a higher one just as well as London had, and superficially Wright and I had much more in common. After all, he was born in Mississippi and spent much time in Memphis, where I was born, and he was a black man. But when I read *Black Boy* or *Uncle Tom's Children*, I was just as cold as when I had read "To Build a Fire." These too were places I had not been.

Later I read as much as I could find by and about Wright. In one macabre passage of an unmemorable work, Wright fills a five-inch paragraph full of names of authors he has read. I will not begin to list them here, but if you are a writer or a reader of writers or, most especially, a scholar, you would recognize many of the names if not their works. I was infuriated when I read this passage.

Richard Wright is actually apologizing for being a writer, attempting to justify his station as a writer, *asking to be accepted* as a writer. Perhaps he didn't know how low that station actually was at the time.

Why, Richard? Why are you explaining to anyone that

you have in fact read all these writers? Do you think this
will please the black people and the white people who
have decided somehow that it is not supposed to be possible for you to be able to write? Don't you see that to some
people you will still be nothing much, nothing but a
mimic doing what you have seen the master do? Why are
you wasting your time with them?

It was very sad for me. Wright had learned he was not
the master. London had learned he was. Until this day, I
cannot see a whit's difference between them as writers,
only in their subject matter and the difference that dic-
tated.

I was angry at Wright for a long time without really
knowing why. And then one day it struck me. Writing is
not something you learn to do. One cannot learn how to
write well. If so, all the so-called great universities would
be turning out great writers all the time. This is not the
case. In fact, many great American writers—and I refuse
to list them for you—had no kind of formal college education to shape them as writers or help them track a straight
course to the top of the middle of the writer's maze. Their
gift is like the gift of a heavy punch to a few boxers.

One can learn how *not* to write. One cannot learn how
to write well. One can only write and hope. Wright did
not need to apologize for being a repository for such bless-
ings, but the world surrounding him, whether he liked it
or not, made this need real to him. No wonder he died an
unseemly, untimely death. He should have died not car-
ing what anyone—other than a few other humans, usually friends, who absolutely slavered over him—thought
of his writing. Who was a better judge than he? Damn
few, let me assure you.

Much as living and becoming an adult had made London into a racist, Wright had become an apologist. He felt
he had to explain how he might have come to have such
talent without stealing it from someone. And he came to
feel this way, damn this world to hell, because of

influences and images and all that was put before him in life.

I make no claims to scholarship in this matter. This is what I think, and I care little for what some think of what I think. The editor of this very collection of essays is a gracious man who once said to me that some of the passages herein seemed to be "almost intellectual." I immediately came back to my hovel to find out where I had gone wrong, to eradicate, if possible, any hint of any sign of intellectualism about these writings. Because writing is not a purely intellectual pursuit, at least not the kind of writing I prefer. Writing is a visceral reenactment of real or imagined history, a recollection and propulsion of projections and observations and sensations, the heavy ammo. And only when it is these things is it in a class unto itself among the arts. Only then is writing a true and singular and irreplacable art form. For only these qualities cannot be replaced by film or music or visual art.

The best works of writing have always been stories taken from life, life both real and imagined, and put down thusly. Soliloquies (like this one) do not cut the mustard. They are not subtle enough. They do not encourage you to draw your own conclusion. I cannot read the editorial pages of newspapers, the op-ed pages as they are called, with much pleasure. I quickly tire of the whippings.

This was the world of Mencken, the world of the op-ed pages. There is good technical writing, writing with few grammatical and spelling errors or slips of syntax and with every word agreeing to some (usually archaic) code, and the transitions of thought and place being as silent as possible. On the op-ed pages, participles do not dangle, negatives do not double, and things usually agree with each other. I would not care if I was ever any good at that kind of writing specifically, for all those things are about nothing much but form. Writing of this type is the clear transmission of thought through an alphabet and that is all it is. It stirs only agreement or disagreement.

True writing stirs so much more. True writing can stir any emotion human beings are capable of feeling or expressing, and that is quite a lot of story. To write with empathy and subtlety is the only rule worthy of adherence within the art.

Mencken gets off the hook with me because he once wrote one great line. I don't particularly care about the rest of his lines. As I have gathered, within my ignorance about the man's work, he was not a particularly strident propagandist for any of his candid views. I have heard that on January 1, 1939, he wrote a column which stated America should provide a haven for the Jewish people of Europe. So he was not the same misanthrope every day, apparently. And besides, when you get right down to it, he might have been a third-rater overall, merely because he thought too highly of himself as a writer and as a human being. Even Mencken could not have been as good as Mencken thought he was.

Besides that, he's dead, for heaven's sake. He's not going to be holding any rallies for racism or sexism or anti-Semitism, and what's more, no one has yet accused him of staging or attending any while he was alive. I will say such writers can lead people by the nose and play fiddler to atrocities, but did not Mencken himself say that when he wrote, "No one ever went broke underestimating the intelligence of the American public?" He didn't seem to be a particularly happy man. Neither did London. Neither did Wright.

After all, writers are the byproducts of the worlds they traverse and soak up. When the Chicago White Sox threw the World Series of 1919—when Mencken was a very young, impressionable man—they were immediately labeled and have been known ever since as the Black Sox, and the number they pulled has been similarly known as the Black Sox scandal.

Now there were no black people anywhere around this

scenario, other than the same as always, cleaning up the messes, knowing what was going to happen ahead of time, being required to take the brunt of the fallout, sweating the small stuff. The owners and gamblers and players involved were white, as were the uniforms, fans, balls, everything. But this became the Black Sox scandal. Just as Ahab's fascination was with the Great White Whale, which is how Mr. Melville entered the back screen door of people's consciousness, at the same time off-spinning the Great White Way, the Great White Hope, the Great White Shark, the Great White House . . . you name it, pretty much.

This is what London and Wright and Mencken and you and I have been inundated with for years, and one small reason why I never cared for *Moby-Dick*. One small reason. Had Mr. Melville's prose been ripping with electricity, had he made me colder, or warmer, I would have been most pleased because, if anything, I read better than I write. But the prose, to me, was turgid and heavy and I live in the latter half of the twentieth century and excuse me but I don't have time for it if it's not moving right along.

So the Great White Whale was just another added technique of repulsion for me since I have learned to be quite aware of any color description which signifies other human traits. Anyone attempting to prop up mores based on this kind of positive-negative color identification is immediately on my B list, with no right of appeal. This happens with the greatest frequency on the editorial pages of the like in which Mencken lurked and which are in the business of pure propaganda, not pure writing. So even though Wright or London were victimized more thoroughly than they might have ever dreamed or dreaded possible, somehow they kept their souls as writers, as far as I have read.

Mencken likely never had such a writer's soul. He was too busy making sure of his subject and verb agreement and his social club roster. I will admit to you right up front that I have many quirks of my own, personal prejudices, paranoias, grudges held both large and small, feelings of ambivalence and rage. My own galaxy is being forged haphazardly from all the cold and heat.

How many people in the world who don't want to be seen as bigots have talked ever so loosely about niggers and shines and shvartzes and kikes and micks and harpies and wops and dagos and krauts and nips and chinks and fags and cunts, or maybe with not quite as much kick as these insults have been insulting just the same, insulting alone or with those like them where they could air with relief their own learned prejudices, and then place the burden of humanity on the backs of others to prove? Who does not have what is called the dark side? Do you see what I mean? When H. L. Mencken's diaries were reviewed by *The Washington Post* and *The New York Times*, one of those periodicals headlined its review thusly:

THE DARK SIDE OF MENCKEN

Is that kind of writing clear enough for you? Do you seem to get it? Do you, dear malleable reader, now think somewhere deep inside yourself that if Mencken evinced some unenviable thoughts and traits, those traits and thoughts are to be seen as part of Mencken's dark half, the black half, *my* half, *your* half, perhaps. Do you see the subtlety, the mind-numbing spirit and life-altering reality of this? Can you sense it in yourselves, how it makes you react, be you black or white or what true blending of colors you are, such as a word in this language can approximate? I do hope after my death all my abominations are chalked up to the Lighter Side of the Great Ebon Wiley. I won't be in a position to care, but it may help another get along.

About Aesthetics

What Black People Won't Eat

If you're frustrated and want to find a way to get into an argument or a fight without actually doing anything wrong, try to get a black person to eat something he or she doesn't want to eat. Then step back and square off.

"Try some of this."

"What is it?"

"Meat."

"What kind of meat?"

"Lamb, I think."

"I don't eat lamb."

"But it's good."

"I said I don't eat lamb."

"Have you ever had lamb?"

"No."

"Then how do you know you don't like it?"

"I didn't say I don't like it. I said I don't eat it. I like my dog, but I wouldn't eat her either. Got any steak?"

If you don't drop the conversation at this point, then you might end up eating a knuckle sandwich. Never assume.

Myself, personally, I don't eat chitterlings or chitlins or

pig offal by any other name. I don't eat caviar. I don't eat
snails. I tried to do without the filthy evil swine entirely
and succeeded for years. Reasonable people, Muslims and
personal experience had convinced me the filthy evil swine
was not meant to be ingested by good and gentle men,
that the filthy evil swine were known to eat anything
from rotten food to dead flies to old shoelaces to fresh
chicken shit, if it was the garnish on slop. I found that if I
ate pork, I suffered headaches. I figured hypertension was
just around the corner. So I swore off the pig for years.

I fell off the wagon one sunny, carefree morning after
smelling bacon frying, then eventually found myself
chomping on ham and pork chops, putting ham hocks in
my collard greens, and eating high and low on the hog in
general.

Even in this new gluttony, if you try to bring me some
chitterlings or some chitlins, you've got problems. Not
only do I not want them, I want to know why you're eating them. You become suspect. I want to know what kind
of person would eat chitterlings/chitlins. All this and I
don't think I've ever even so much as tasted a chitterling/
chitlin in my life. But I don't want them. I have smelled
them cooking.

I've tasted caviar. I doubt if I ever will again. People
say the best foods are an acquired taste. That might or
might not be true, but caviar isn't food. Well, it might be
food to a frog, or to a starving Russian, but it isn't food to
me. Caviar is fish eggs. I'm for letting the eggs grow up to
be fish first. Then I'll eat them. But eating the fish as
eggs—not only is it not mouth-watering, it doesn't even
sound fair. I've got more pride and taste than a frog.

The only eggs I'll eat are chicken eggs, and they'd
better not look funny or they're out the window.

We won't even discuss snails.

Black people won't eat other people, no matter how
well done they are. As far as I know, cannibalism came
and went with the Donner Party, although cannibalism is

still a joke for darker people who live in the tropics. Lighter people come in and make movies and documentaries about darker people and ask them if they or some of their forebears might have been cannibals. This makes for a good documentary. Alas, this is kind of like saying the Indians scalped the cowboys in the Old West.

Actually, it was the Indian scalps that were fetching a good price with the general stores and the fur traders. I'm sure the Indians were completely shocked the first time they found one of their fellows dead and minus the top of his head. But if the cowboys are peerless at anything, it is public relations.

Peter Minuit "bought" Manhattan for twenty-eight dollars and sixty-four beads, or vice versa. Well, the native who "sold" it to him probably was laughing as much as Peter. Oh, you want to buy this land that has been here all along? Sure. Now if Peter had said, "I want to buy the right to keep you off this land," then the native might have told him that right was not for sale.

So the Indians became the scalpers in the movies, and the darker people became the cannibals in the documentaries, even though no darker people were in the Donner Party. None were left in the end, at least.

But there's always a black person around somewhere, where you'd least expect it, even in a group like the Donner Party. None of them would have known the black person was there until the party decided to fix up Ingrid for dinner. And the black person probably said, "No way am I eating that—er—her," and gave himself away. After that he was dessert.

Black people have a reputation for frying food and eating fried foods. Myself, personally, I am a willing martyr on that particular cross. Fried chicken eggs that look right, fried chicken, fried green tomatoes, fried fish, fried okra, fried potatoes. If you are entertaining me and I don't eat what you're having and you have nothing else, there is no sense in talking about it. Try frying whatever it

is you have. I probably won't eat it, but I might say it
sort of smells good and be content with cheese and crack-
ers. And you will have fulfilled your obligation as host.

Location has a lot to do with what black people will
and won't eat. Black or white, if you are in the South,
you are going to eat anything that's put in front of you, if
you've got any (1) brains or (2) home training. If a female
relative of yours in the South has taken the time to make
something to eat—and believe me, she has—then you
must have the decency to eat it or be socially ostracized.
Of course, in the South it is usually no problem obliging
the cooks. Whatever they prepare, you are likely to want
to eat it or at least smell it. Southern black women burn,
baby.

Black athletes have a different eating pattern. I can
remember when I was a boy, after football practice I
would eat anything in the kitchen that didn't have legs or
an electrical cord attached. Sure enough, many years later
the football coach at Howard University, Willie Jeffries,
gained fame and notoriety during the 1987 season not
because his team had nine wins and only one loss, but
because he said the following about his players, who
featured an offensive line which averaged a svelte 320
pounds per man: "When we go to a restaurant, we don't
get a menu—we get an estimate."

The two great prizefighters, Sugar Ray Robinson and
Muhammad Ali, were eating dinner one evening. Robin-
son ordered up some center-cut pork chops. Ali, the
Muslim, was taken aback, but he was nevertheless polite.
Robinson was his ring progenitor, his fistic hero. It pained
Ali to see Robinson eating something Ali himself would
never eat. Especially the filthy evil swine. When
Robinson's dish arrived, Ali pointed at the steaming pork
and said, "Do you know what will happen to you if you
eat those?"

Robinson said, "I know what'll happen if I don't."

"What?" Ali asked.

"I'll be hungry," Sugar Ray said.

The one thing you can be sure that a black person will never eat is his or her own tongue.

Why Black People
Have No Culture

Black people have no culture because most of it is out on loan to white people. With no interest.

Music? Let's just say if it weren't for black people, there's no telling what we'd have to listen to each day. Instead, music is rich and enduring, and we can listen to whatever makes us happy and allows us to get by. You don't think Elvis Presley thought it up by himself? Chuck Berry came down from St. Louis and helped Elvis out. Presley saw Chuck and became Elvis. After he saw how it was done, it was as simple as one-two-three.

Elvis wasn't popular among some white people at first. Usually, older white men. They made propaganda films warning the public of Presley's "nigraisms" that if left unchecked would pollute—well, you know what they would pollute. Now older white men will look to kill you if you say something bad about Elvis Presley.

Whatever music isn't popular at the time it first comes out, you can be certain black people came up with it and nobody else is quite ready for it. I have estimated the world will be ready for the finest avant-garde jazz in the middle twenty-first century.

Once white people borrow it for a while, the music

takes off. Ragtime, blues, rhythm, big-band, reggae, gospel, rap, do-wop, lesser forms of jazz, go-go, hip-hop, forms within classical, forms within country, you name it, black people play it, live it, write it, thought it up, helped think it up or inspired it. Roll over, Beethoven, and tell us where your people were from. Say hello to Lester Young and John Coltrane while you're up. Not that white people don't have their originators and supreme technicians and instrument virtuosos. They just don't have all of them. Mozart, for example, was the master of the note. Beethoven, on the other hand, was the master of the emotion the note can muster. Creativity is at the root of all forms of music, which is why black people are so adept at it. Creative is black people's middle name. If necessity is the mother of invention, there is no doubt necessity is also a sister.

Speech? Why, it amazes some black people—specifically, me—to hear white people mumble snidely about the way black people are known to talk, with ever-widening dialectal form, then hear the same white people do their level best to talk the same talk about two years later. Mark Twain with Tom Sawyer and Huck Finn was aware of this predilection. Those are two of the great novels of American history—even white people say this—and they were written in dialect. From then to right on to chill out to you got that right to you know it. You can watch a film where there isn't a black person in sight, just some young white people, and if you closed your eyes, you'd swear you were on the corner of 125th Street and Malcolm X Boulevard. High and low fives all over the place.

Art? That's another story. People thought Picasso was out of his mind to study what few African artifacts were left by the beginning of this century. Some people claimed there weren't many to begin with. Picasso looked at what little was left and, being a great artist, immediately knew better. This was not the work of beginners. These folks had been at this for a while. So Picasso kept his mouth shut and did what he did best. He painted. Picasso came out with cubism and the whole world was agog. What an innovator.

And Picasso said, you know it.

Speaking of these kinds of art, I must pause to make a sober point. Of all the great sculptures of the first Golden Age of the Pyramids none had survived intact because all the noses have been defaced. The sculpture of Amenemhet III (1843 B.C.) has no nose. The nose has been chiseled or blasted off. The same with the Great Sphinx of Gizeh. The same with Amenemhet II. Kemet was the world leader of culture—artistic, literary, technological, you name it—of this time. I know of no other leading culture whose artifacts were so callously debased and defaced by later visitors, even if those visitors were of a destructive mind and bent.

Usually, human beings respect their art even while they are killing each other over it. They respect its power. It was as if whoever defaced these artifacts believed they could somehow change history, and perhaps they were right, in a shallow manner of speaking. What they could change was the perception of history. That is all. What was, was. Any look at the artifacts of the Shang Dynasty of China (1766–1022 B.C.) would reveal the Negroid features most clearly. In what is now known as Mexico, the Aztecs referred to a preceding impressive group of visitors as the Totonac, "the people of the warm land." The Totonac were preceded by the Olmec civilization (150 B.C.) which current Mexican scholars have identified as being greatly influenced by the Egyptian-Nubian culture. The Tajín Head figurine of the Totonac (A.D. 250) escaped defacement, and exists today in all its marble magnificance. It looks a little like a rendering of Louis Armstrong.

Style? Josephine Baker left St. Louis and went to France, where they told her she was the most stylish thing going. And the French don't give up the style points so easily. She sang, entertained and entwined men's souls around her sensuous fingers, like Scheherazade or Cleopatra or Sheba. Then she was with the French Resistance during World War II. Other entertainers, like Maurice Chevalier, had to explain why they were entertaining German troops during that time. Josephine had a style all her own. Even other black people couldn't imitate it. Diana Ross was supposedly going to star in a movie about Josephine's life, but the reception from the people who used to watch Josephine was so cool, Diana just let it drop for a while. But Diana wasn't bad herself, stylewise. She just wasn't Josephine Baker. Closest you could get, according to white people, was Marilyn Monroe. And to think, black people always figured it might be a Lena Horne or a Dorothy Dandridge. Marilyn's great skills as an entertainer were dying her hair blond, making kissy lips at the camera, and acting like she was a ditz when she wasn't. Marilyn was smart enough to know what the people, especially the older white men, wanted. But she was no Josephine Baker, either. She just got more ink.

Ink? White people seem to think they have black people there, because it is said there are no books and tablets among historical artifacts in equatorial Africa. This is suspicious because if they had found some, who's to say white people would have let everybody else know? What were a few scrolls going to hurt? We've already seen what happened to the noses on the faces of the pharaohs of the Golden Age.

Now, let's assume there weren't any books written in equatorial Africa. Say the storytellers, *griots* and gossiping housewives took care of the whole business. What about nonequatorial Africa? Black people lived on the coast, too, you know. In a few ways, Africa was no different than anyplace else. If you went to Kansas or Nebraska and asked where all the writers were, the people there would say they've all gone to the coast. Well, there were people in Africa too. And the strange African people, the ones who would turn out to be writers and artists, they all left the central country and went to the coast. They were encouraged to go, since sitting down creating art wasn't and isn't considered an honest day's work in the heartland.

So, if you went to central Africa, as white anthropologists did, and asked the farmers who lived there, "Where are your writers and other strange folks?" the farmers and peasants would tell you, "Why, they all went to the coast. They come back to visit now and then. Them that's left." If you asked the farmers where all their books were, they'd probably tell you the same. If you wanted some food or some advice, they could help you. The white people who first visited must not have been anthropologists, or in much of an asking mood.

A classic example of this cavalier brushing aside of the obvious would be illustrated by the fate of the imposing and ancient Great Zimbabwe colossus, the largest and most impressive ruins south of Egypt on the continent of Africa. Of the ruins that are left, of course. The Great Zimbabwe is an old place of thought and consideration. It has a conical watchtower and granite walls and enclosures, with observation points, hidden passageways, broad plazas and high-ceilinged rooms, which were once laced with art and artifacts of the highest and oldest order. This magnificent place was obviously built by the people who lived around Zimbabwe, since the ruins, nine centuries old at least, are some two hundred miles south of Harare. And Zimbabwe is in central Africa, the very place where the white people who first came there said no writers, much less any civilized people, had ever lived.

While the British colonized Zimbabwe, and called it Rhodesia, the thinking by this mother country's eminent archeologists and paleontologists and anthropologists and especially its racists was that no African people could have created such a grand and ancient monument as the Great

Zimbabwe, the "House of Chiefs," even though the indig-
enous Shona people—some of those very farmers who
weren't supposed to be able to do anything sophisticated
like write—looked around and shook their heads and kept
them bowed and waited for this too to pass.

The awe-inspiring, highly intelligent, self-loving, narcissistic and very destructive colonialists took note of this
by writing it down. "No African built those walls except
under expert foreign guidance," wrote a Brit named H.
Maclear Bate in a 1940 report entitled "Report from the
Rhodesia." Another man, Peter Garlake, wrote in 1973
that "to [people like Bate], the African simply had not the
energy, will, organization, foresight or skill to build those
walls. Indeed, he appeared so backward that it seemed
that his entire race could never have accomplished the
task at any period." Such is an example of the power of
writing. It is little wonder that all the evidence to the
contrary, from paintings to writings to gold and silver
sculpture, was hauled away by treasure hunters from
Europe from its "discovery" in 1928 by a Boer, of all people, named Adam Renders, until it was deemed protected
by law by the British government. Up until then, any
treasure belonged to them anyway—a bad rationalization
for yet another attempt to change and destroy history.

Meanwhile, all kinds of books and tablets and scrolls
and stories were written around the coast of Africa, and a
lot of ships left from there for distant ports. So Africa
ended up in Russia, with Aleksandr Pushkin, who is called
the father of Russian literature. Africa came to France,
where Alexandre Dumas was that nation's most prolific
writer. His son wrote the greatest love story in French
literature, *Camille*. The House of Dumas is a particular
revelation to me because it ties up the entire question of
culture and who has it and who doesn't, under one roof.

Alexandre Dumas *père* was the son of one Thomas
Dumas, a soldier-general, rider, swordsman and swash-
buckler of great physical strength ﹐ and extreme

handsomeness. By the end of the eighteenth century, he had risen to the rank of general in Napoleon Bonaparte's army by sheer force of skill and presence. When Napoleon invaded Egypt, it appears that there was at least one dissenting voice among his generals, that of Thomas Dumas. Dumas questioned the motives of this invasion, and his suspicions were borne out after Napoleon's artillery was responsible for one of the most heinous acts of history, blowing the nose off the Sphinx.

Napoleon and some of his generals just couldn't handle these great works of immense size and antiquity looking more like Thomas Dumas than Napoleon Bonaparte. Of course Dumas was accused of mutiny, as well documented later by historians such as Francis Gribble, W. R. Phipps and Guy Endore. General Dumas was refused honorable retirement, back pay and pension by Napoleon.

Dumas died prematurely, but not without leaving two children, one of them Alexandre. And to look at some of his works—*The Three Musketeers, The Count of Monte Cristo,* and especially *The Man in the Iron Mask,* one cannot escape the fact that Alexandre's inspiration was his magnificent father. Dumas wrote his history as a fiction, a great series of fictions, and in that way it was preserved. It was preserved as long as the likes of an Errol Flynn could play the title roles. But that was not the truth. That was not the history. That was not what was.

Alexandre's son, Dumas *fils,* wrote but one major work. That work just happened to be *Camille,* which, in fact, may be the greatest love story ever written or told in any language, with the probable exception of Homer's *Iliad* and *Odyssey.* Even the critics then might have agreed with this assessment, as long as they didn't realize the Dumases were what would be called black people here in America, and that the D'Artagnans and counts and Marguerites of which they wrote were—in the minds of the authors—precisely as they were, of a claimed and understood African descent in great or small fraction.

Africa lifted her literary head again in Brazil, in Machado de Assis and Mario de Andrade, and in America, where Zora Neale Hurston was born to write. Zora Neale Hurston and Mark Twain are the best American writers as far as I am concerned. Zora first came along during the Harlem Renaissance. Black writers and poets and artists and photographers were everywhere. Langston Hughes, Countee Cullen, Claude McKay, Romare Bearden, James Van Der Zee, Scipio Moorehead, Edward Bannister, Edmonia Lewis, Henry Tanner, Meta Warrick Fuller, May Howard Jackson, Hale Woodruff, Sargent Johnson, Jacob Lawrence, James Cozzens, Grace Lumpkin, Lillian Smith, Evelyn Scott, William Gardiner Smith, Frank Yerby, Ralph Ellison, Willard Motley, etc. And to those I do not know or mention, I do a disservice. Zora Neale Hurston was a particular favorite of mine. That's my dance, of course.

Dance? I've got a feeling there are two kinds up in the Bronx or Brooklyn who never tie their sneakers because they're too busy using them, inventing every single contemporary dance that has come out in the last eighty years. First they invent the haircut, then the dance to go with it.

Drama? Paul Robeson certainly wasn't what Shakespeare had in mind when he penned *Othello*, eh? Paul had a bass on him, didn't he? He could carry luggage with that voice. And I'm told he couldn't hold a candle next to Ira Aldridge.

Marian Anderson. Aretha Franklin. Minnie Riperton. Patti LaBelle. Sarah Vaughan. Jessye Norman. Miss Ella Fitzgerald. Chaka Khan. Dinah Washington. Anita Baker. Mahalia Jackson. Phyllis Hyman. Leontyne Price. That would be a choir fit for any religion.

Religion? Well, it seems the only aspect of culture black people are given historical credit for by white people is the uniqueness of our church service and the reverence of our reverends. The irony is that this is just about the only thing black people have borrowed. If you're a missionary, preacher, minister or priest, black people love you—as black people love all people—even though you do not necessarily happen to be deserving of such treatment. You could be the biggest cur on the face of the earth, but if you know how to say "the power of Gawt" with the proper intensity and inflection, black people will assume you're fine.

Black people come as Muslim, Jehovah's Witness, Seventh-Day Adventist, Catholic, Protestant, even Jewish, African Methodist Episcopalian, Colored, er, Christian Methodist Episcopalian, Baptist, Colored Baptist and more. In most of these cases, it was black people who borrowed the idea from white people, with one of the exceptions being the Colored Baptists, who had to get up and show white Baptists what a Baptist was supposed to be like. In some parts of Haiti and other places, one unique black church service is called *voudon,* which some people, black and white, have attempted to portray as a kind of abominable witchcraft.

All religions are abominations when they cause death. No Crusades have been fought over *voudon.* Some of these same people who talk about Haiti and *voudon* will go right along eating their sanctified bread and drinking their sanctified wine while the priest or minister is saying, "Take the body, drink the blood of your Savior."

But don't rush to knock *voudon.* In twenty years, who knows what you might have to believe in order to get by?

If you want to be prepared and find out what's down early, go to St. Louis, Brooklyn, France or the coast of Africa and find the black people who are not glassy-eyed from being confused for so long. Find these black people and ask them for the vanguard. They'll tell you what it is.

Integration and Desegregation

What do you get out of integration?

I'll tell you what you get.

When Central High School in Little Rock, Arkansas, was integrated in 1957, a lot of white people got very ugly in the face about it. Some of them carry wrinkles and lines of disfigurement in their faces until this very day, from the pain that the very idea of integration caused them. Some ten children from a "segregated" black high school were going to go to Central, come hell or high water. I have seen film of these children as they were interviewed during these days of change. They were bright, spoke evenly to the camera, made their thoughts sound brave and communicated well. They all did reasonably well later in life.

Now, after thirty years of integration, what do you get? You get teachers who just want to get the day done. You get ballplayers who couldn't form a compound sentence to keep a dog off them. They wind up either snookered out of their professional wages, if they get that far, or in drug rehabilitation. You now have high schools where guns and knives and other items of mayhem are parts of the dress code. You still have "segregated" black schools, but those bright, smart children are gone from there, along with the bright, smart teachers, gone to the integrated school, which has become a suburban academy. That's what you get with integration.

What do you get out of integration?

You get so-called "integrated" school systems where the white principals and teachers cannot accept the fact that there are gifted and talented black children. So the exceptional black child becomes either "too boisterous" or "hyperactive" or something else even worse. He couldn't just be bright. Not in this integrated situation. It would make the white kids uncomfortable if he were a little bit smarter than some of them. It would go against the institutional framework of racism, under which we have all been raised. It would cause dissonance in the hum of the engine of institutional racism.

With integration, black students are the only ones who get the feeling they somehow don't belong. The irony of all this is that the white children were the ones who were in the segregated schools all along. Any black child who was not blind and went to a so-called "segregated" black school could look around and see that a certain portion of the school population was black, a certain portion was brown, a certain portion was tan, a certain portion was high tan, what the old people once called yellow, and a certain portion was all but white. They were not called white, but this is the way they appeared to the eye.

But since the children in the "segregated" black school were told they were all the same, very nearly, you only had the usual rigors of adolescence to put up with, and not all the adult framework of racism to make life even harder. (Black children never got the idea they were not what they were supposed to be until integration.)

What else do you get with integration?

I'll tell you what you get.

A man named Oscar Micheaux once made films that

had black attorneys, black doctors, black property owners, and handsome black heroes and ne'er-do-wells in
them. With integration, you get films with ugly black
pimps, pinheaded drug dealers, bum jocks, lovesick
singers, junkies, a few genius black comics and some stupid black clowns, none of whom are allowed to have any
decent feelings about each other, or even kiss. That's what
you get.

What do you get out of integration?

I'll tell you what you get.

You get suspected of everything. Every time you earn
something, somebody gave it to you. Every time you work
hard for something, you're a natural. Every time you
show merit, the rules on merit are altered to make them
more obtuse.

What do you get out of integration?

I'll tell you what you get.

You get the sizzle and not the steak.

You get a lot of people fired or demoted. The woods
once were full of black committee chairmen, black teachers, black principals. With integration, they are all assistant something or other. Those mentioned above are considered rarities, even by many young black people, who
don't know any better because they haven't been taught
any better.

What do you get with integration?

You get chaos among young people who don't know any
better because they don't know that they can be any
better. You get the decline of every single black institution, from private black colleges and universities to black
social groups, to families and entire communities. You get
the decline of every single one of them but the church,
and if you're not careful, even that's only a matter of
time.

Black people once raised each other's children. Each
child might have been your child. That's how children
were supposed to be treated. With integration, you get

people who don't know who their neighbors are and don't
particularly care for the children of those neighbors. You
get black people who believe the terms *upper class, middle
class* and *lower class* apply to them, so they treat each
other's children accordingly, and eventually the children
treat each other accordingly. That's what you get with
integration.

What do you get with integration?

I'll tell you what you get.

You get people who are acting as much as living.

What do you get with integration?

I'll tell you what you get.

You get disrespected, misrepresented, passed over for
promotion, jokes told about you that aren't even funny, a
ceiling placed over your ambitions, a precarious niche,
some unnecessary heartache, an unshakable disquiet and a
slightly bigger paycheck.

What do you get with desegregation?

I'll tell you what you get.

You get a choice. You can go where you please for business or pleasure, but you don't *have* to go anywhere. And
when you go to do business, if the terms are unacceptable, you can take your business elsewhere. With desegregation, you have the right to go anywhere, but you don't
have to go just for the sake of going. Who wants to stand
around a bunch of people who don't want to be there,
with no pleasure or business to gain, with nothing in
mind but the proximity of the other people? With
desegregation there is a choice.

What do you get with desegregation?

You get self-reliance, because desegregation doesn't
mean somebody else is going to fight your battles for you.

With desegregation, you suddenly gain the notion that
your idea might not be bad after all. You gain leadership.

With desegregation, you realize you don't have to play
football or basketball or sing or be a comic in order to do
something useful in the society. You gain confidence.

With desegregation, you get self-respect, because no one respects a chicken-heart who stands around begging to be liked and accepted when the person he's standing around has said he doesn't want to see you standing around anymore, wanting to be liked and respected and being so chicken-hearted about it. With desegregation, you have your own. You have the opportunity for entrepreneurship if you're up to it. With desegregation, you feel more up to it.

With desegregation, you get positive feedback, an idea of your skills and market, a will and eventually a way. With desegregation you get a challenge, pride, the same services and options everyone else has, peace of mind and a somewhat smaller check.

With desegregation you find out less is more and that you can do it. You must. Now. Which would you choose?

Who Black People
Don't Like

Black people have a high tolerance for everybody except themselves. Black people don't like other black people. Some of the worst bigots in the world against dark people are dark people. White people once held the top spot in this category and set the records for it. But now white people spend a lot of time pining for the good old days, while black people help put racism into social practice.

All the official explaining and theorizing in the world does not explain this phenomenon to me. People have tried. They have told me this in-house racism has to do with the outhouse racism black people have suffered. The tendency for self-destruction stems from a history of being destroyed. It wouldn't be right if black people weren't catching hell. So during the slow periods when white people are too busy making money, worrying about the dollar and waxing nostalgic to bother black people, we give hell to ourselves.

The most demeaning racial utterances against black people I have ever heard firsthand have come out of the mouths of black people. At least white people who were racist would usually wait until I wasn't around. I am ashamed to say that some of these insults have even come out of the mouths of some of my relatives. This tells me I have been infected in some way as well. If a white person had innocently shared with me what some black people have innocently shared with me, I would have gone down swinging. As it was, I could only stand there, amazed, and nod.

Some light-skinned black people are prejudiced against dark people. Some dark-skinned black people are even worse in their prejudice against dark people and light people. They have no one to pass the hate down to, so they absorb it, then hand it back over. Those lips, that color, that part of town. All these different-colored black-on-black racists wanted me to know it had nothing to do with them, though they were compelled to comment.

I once met a woman who was brown. She had become enlightened. She had those lips, but she understood full lips were the best kind for her to have. Maybe it was because the white woman movie stars had begun to have those lips. I don't know. But my enlightened brown friend still was sensitive about noses. I like noses. I think everyone should have one, if possible. My brown friend asked me if I found something wrong with the African nose. I asked her if she thought there was but one type of nose in all the history of Africa. Had she seen the films of the starving children in Ethiopia? Did they all have the same nose? Did they look as if they cared either way? My friend believed a caricature.

"African-Americans are one of the most genetically diverse people in the world," according to Dr. Michael Blakey, an anthropologist and sociologist at Howard University in Washington. "An African mixture, a European mixture, and a Native American mixture which derives ultimately from Asia. We are a distinctly diverse people."

All well and good for Dr. Blakey, but why is it that black people who are not anthropologists don't see this?

Whenever you hear a lot of teeth-sucking among black people, you know that some black person who was a little too black or a little too light or a little too brown has cornered some success, or let everybody down by letting success elude them even though they gave it a good long try. There are people who are said to "think they're something," according to the black people who are sucking their teeth. And yes, those people probably do think they're something.

White people? Most white people can't touch black people when it comes to prejudice against black people. White people just wrote the book on it. It is the black people who have perfected the technique in everyday practice. Some white people bend over backward to make black people feel comfortable. And black people will take anything from them but authority. It's not a fact unless black people hear it from very thin lips. It's not real unless a white person has confirmed it.

I learned the folly of this by writing. When I wrote, invariably some white person would tell me that it wasn't good writing. If I believed it, I wouldn't have written another word. Black people have this knack of agreeing with all of white people's assessments, as if white people couldn't be mistaken, jealous, envious or just plain wrong sometimes, just like black people. Black people go on believing, which is why black people don't like black people. White people always said it was for the best.

You'd think that black people in college would have learned better. But no. In college, black people join fraternities and sororities. I joined a fraternity myself. I met good people. But it seemed fraternities and sororities gave some people another excuse not to like other people in other fraternities and sororities. And the people not in the fraternities and sororities didn't care for any of us.

Some black people don't like black people and quote statistics to back themselves up. They are popular at cocktail parties. Dr. Thomas Sowell and Mr. Roy Innis, for example. Dr. Sowell is a scholar and a theorist. In spite of this, he says the occasional sensible thing. Mr. Roy Innis is Mr. Roy Innis. Dr. Sowell is always turning up at some university or in some newspaper, talking in impressive academese about how black people can't do this and won't do that. Invariably, he is telling this to white people. It seems you cannot be a scholar without going by white people first. Not surprisingly, Dr. Sowell's opinions about and charges against black people make him popular and quotable among white people. Dr. Sowell probably thinks it's his own brilliance that causes him to be so popular. I've got news for him. It's his act.

Any white racist knows he can't do that job any better than a black one. Take Roy Innis of the Congress on Racial Equality. Mr. Innis lives in New York. When a sick twerp named Goetz shot four black people on a subway, Mr. Innis was the first person in line to say that this was the right thing to do. Suddenly Mr. Innis was on television and quoted in all the right newspapers. Here was a man of depth. That was the implication. Why else would he be on television? If Mr. Innis had said this shooting of black people might be questionable behavior, he wouldn't have gotten twenty seconds of airtime. But at least Mr. Innis doesn't whisper.

I have heard black people downgrade the black doctor or the black lawyer, as if they'd rather trust white people to get them well or serve them justice. This makes sense if you're black or Alice in Wonderland. Black people don't slant the news to their liking, deliver the cigarettes to the black community in bulk, lock up the economy in their favor, or ship drugs by air. Black people just treat each other like they do.

Murder is the acid test of dislike. Black people pass with flying colors. Black people will kill each other rather quickly, and over the most simple things. The things are so inconsequential to a life that you know black people aren't really killing themselves over these things. They're killing themselves because they don't like each other.

In Washington, D.C., in January of 1988, thirty-six people were murdered, the vast majority of them black. If the vast majority of these murdered had been white, you can bet white people would have had a meeting or two and there would have been an accounting for it. Most black people merely sighed and said it was too bad. One black high school child was murdered for his portable tape player. White people called this a "ghetto blaster." Supposedly responsible black people took the cue and hated the ghetto blaster with a passion, while white people went out and bought them by the gross to sell them to the black people who thought they hated them until they saw the white people were selling them. Then they became precious. This boy was killed over his.

Another teenager was killed over his jacket. He wouldn't give up his jacket to a bully because he had worked for it. This logic didn't stop the robbery and murder from occurring. It probably infuriated the robber and murderer even more. Black people weren't supposed to work for what they had. Didn't this boy know any better? Two lives ruined for the price of one self-hate.

The biggest single reason why I know for a fact that black people don't like black people is the drug trade.

Drugs have always been around. Religion is the opiate of the masses, Karl Marx is supposed to have said. Well, Karl, around here, opiate is the opiate of the masses. Earlier in the twentieth century, the same affliction happened to the Chinese, and in China, no less. There were signs over businesses in China which said, "No Dogs or Chinese Allowed." Now, this was *in* China. I told you before, white people set all the records for racism. Anyway, a few of the Chinese weren't happy about the fact that along with these signs, white people were bringing boatloads of opium and heroin into China so that the Chinese couldn't care less what the signs said, as long as they could leave this cruel world for a few hours with the opium pipe.

A few Chinese got together and asked the white people in charge to stop the boats full of opium from coming to China. They could work out something with the signs later on.

There was a double-sided profit in the opium for the white people, however. Not only could they charge for the opium, it would serve to keep the Chinese people inside and out of the way. Eventually, a few Chinese got the message. Luckily for the Chinese, there are so many of them that a few of them actually works out to be a few million. Then there was a rebellion, and soon no more opium-laden ships came to China. This was for the best, all things considered.

In America, a few black people is only a few black people. But the same situation exists. We know this because white people have said it. It must be true. Francis Ford Coppola, in his movie *The Godfather*, had one of his Mafia characters come right out and say, "I'd keep [drugs] among the darker people, the coloreds. They're animals anyway, so let them lose their souls."

Black people couldn't expect white people to just stop transporting drugs, not considering the double-sided profit. So the course for a person who likes himself would be to avoid the drug and the admission of self-hate. Cut off the demand, there is no need for supply. Supply will rot, and this will be for the best.

This is easier said than done when every type of drug can be found on every street corner and you don't like yourself to begin with and only want to leave this cruel world for a little while. Some black people have lived so long with the specter of drugs hanging over their lives, they wouldn't know what to do without them. They would have to learn that their lives could be better and they'd have more time to spend on the worthwhile things, like developing a healthy affinity for themselves.

Many of the times when black people kill black people, drugs are at the bottom of it. Some of the people doing the killing and dying call themselves businessmen, like the goombah in *The Godfather*. And they are. They are in the business of not liking black people. And they are on the retail side of that.

On January 22, 1989, five black people, most of them Jamaican nationals, were killed across the street from Landover Mall in Landover, Maryland, just outside Washington. They were killed over a drug deal gone bad. "They don't mess around," said Major James Ross of the Prince Georges County police to *The Washington Post*. He spoke of Jamaicans involved in the drug-related killing. "If you steal their drugs or hold back on their money, they go after you."

Indeed, they all go after you, from the Godfather on down.

Now there are many people out there who will say that all this is paranoia and that drug use is an individual's choice and it just so happens that more black people choose this way. I happen to know better. I happen to know that it's a setup. And if it isn't, I prefer to think that way because it keeps me on my toes.

In late 1989, *USA Today* conducted a study of available FBI data and concluded that black people were being arrested at a rate far out of proportion to their drug use in America. American University criminologist James Lynch went so far as to say that although drug use was broad-based in American society, "the enforcement falls on the underclass." Falls like a grand piano from the top of the Empire State Building is what it does. A black cabdriver from Brooklyn was tooling down the New Jersey Turnpike one fine day early in 1989, when he was pulled over by a New Jersey state trooper, who was white. The black driver was briefly at a loss as to why he was stopped. At least, that's what he told his fares. But he also knew deep in his mind that he might be stopped at any time, for no reason at all. At any rate, one of the officers inspected his car and pulled a couple of ounces of cocaine from beneath his front seat. The black cab driver was incredulous, but this didn't stop him from spending thirty days in the slammer, for no other reason than that he was black and these officers of the law could get away with taking cocaine from the evidence piles which the police are always holding. They could then set him up and give themselves a gold star on their rating for this kind of nonsense.

According to one Mike Taibbi, a conscientious television reporter in New York, arrest records show that a black man has a 1,500 percent greater chance of being stopped for whatever reason on the New Jersey Turnpike than a white driver would. How do you like those odds?

Furthermore, this cocaine was still in circulation. It went right back into the confiscated police supply. By now, the police in most major cities should have enough supplies to fill several tall silos. And the funny thing is, whenever the police have one of these large-volume busts, they never mention any people. If they get ten million dollars' worth of cocaine, with a street value of five hundred million dollars, or whatever, they always show the cocaine sitting guiltily in its tan and biege packaging. But they never show the people they arrested in connection with these large busts. If they caught any humans along with all this guilty cocaine, we never hear about it.

I suspect this is because damn few black people are moving that kind of volume. If it's a small bust, and a black man is involved, you get his entire résumé on television. If it's a big bust, the two thousand zillion tons of cocaine got here on its own. So if black people don't like black people, it's easy to see why. We're trying to agree with the system.

The next time someone offers you drugs, you can thank him if you want, but if you take the drug, you are just an accessory to your own destruction. Better to thumb your nose at the people who don't like you, whether they are aware that they don't like you or not. Better to look in a mirror and admire what you find. Damn who or what people say they like. If you were good enough for God, you ought to be good enough for you. You *are* God, in your own way. When you're black, this information might come as a shock. You will get over it in time. You might even start to like the idea.

Who Black People Trust

Every so often I am greatly amused to read a feature story or psychological study about a black subject, written by a white author who will make some mention of this black person "not trusting whites." The black person's perceived lack of trust comes off like some kind of character flaw. My uncle Charles always said to "Trust yet not a living soul; walk even carefully among the dead." And I always considered this salient advice. Trust is a gift hard earned.

Pity the poor one who by nature trusts all people, no matter what color they are. Why would a black person be suspect for not trusting some white person he or she just met? Given historical facts, it is a wonder any black people trust any white people further than around the corner. And, either way, what does it matter? If two people are getting married then, yes, they should trust each other. Other than that, trust is a matter of catch as catch can.

Let's put the shoe on the other foot. Many times I've ridden an elevator with a white person who suddenly became nervous upon finding me there. I know this has to roll off my back like water if I want to keep the small bit of sanity I depend on to keep me afloat in a world which does not trust me merely on face value. And I really don't even look that bad.

So why should any white person be somehow offended because he or she isn't trusted by me? Why should that make me suspect? Why?

Because everybody wants to be respected enough to be trusted. Only white people assume they deserve this respect just because they are white and want it. The truth is simple. Black people have to love you before they trust you—and then it's iffy. This has nothing to do with color or preference. It all depends on you.

Hard experience has taught black people this: Only those you know and trust can truly hurt you to the quick in this life. You expect to be hurt by everybody else.

Sun

The sun is my flag. All others are temporary. Only that flag in the sky was here when the dinosaurs were out there cabbage-patching, having all the best of it while lording over everything and everybody, not needing to pay attention to their p's and q's. What distant cousins of men were around at the time stayed in the water, well out of the dinosaurs' way. Over the earth reigned the flag of the sun, and the reptiles carried their flags in their jaws. If they could have spoken English, they would have called their flags "teeth." They were more honest than men.

The dinosaurs fought among themselves for a few tens of thousands of years until the sun was taken from them for a short while by what intellectuals now say was some great cosmic accidental upheaval of nature that had nothing to do with God. The mighty dinosaurs could do nothing without the sun but die. Even their teeth rotted eventually.

Now men rule over the earth. They fight and argue about which man is mightier and which flag will rule. In a place temporarily called Alabama, State Representative Thomas Reed, a black man, went to try and take down the Confederate flag from atop the state capitol in

Montgomery in February of 1988. The governor of Alabama, Guy Hunt, a white man, had Representative Reed and eleven other men who wanted to take down the flag arrested by white police, who can be to black men what tyrannosaurus rex was to dinosaurs.

This Confederate flag was around 130 years old when Representative Reed tried to take it down. It stood for oppression to him. To Governor Hunt, it was a symbol of power lording over everything and everybody. So the two men fought. It does not matter that they fought in a civilized manner, not to the sun. The sun does nothing but shine on. It is all happening in 150 years, the space of less than a second by the sun's time. Men have determined the length of the sun's life expectancy, and they probably aren't off by more than two or three million years.

We'll never know.

Why is the sun my flag? Simple. First, a story.

My first experience with the Confederate flag came when I was but a boy, much more interested in dinosaurs and girls than the missteps of men. I went to the circus one day with my class, the circus is the last remaining approximation of the Mesozoic Age around these days, outside the veld. I think I was eight or nine years old. The circus was wonderful to me then, I remember that, although I cannot remember any of the acts. I only remember the whole experience warmly.

My friends and schoolmates and I sat together, little black children as I would later find out. At the time, we were just children. My wonderful mother had given me three dollars with which to find food and perhaps a small souvenir at the circus. Gaunt vendors snaked through our small party, hawking their cheap wares. Among their trinkets were small flags of two types; the American flag, by this time fifty stars worth, and the Confederate flag. For some reason, the hawkers pressed the Confederate flags on us, and I, always a fool, bought one for fifty cents.

I suppose this makes my group seem naïve, even though

we were eight or nine years old. Even then we should
have had some idea of history. But our instructors, I suppose, had more important things to teach us up until that
point. We were in the third grade. I only know that I
walked home in a dark blue car coat, with my Confederate flag fluttering mightily in the autumn breeze.

When I arrived home, I went directly to the back
room, which was the bedroom for three boys. I tacked my
flag on the wall above and behind the tiny gas heater. I
stood back and admired my handiwork. Then my mother
entered the room. She had resided off and on in the South
for a much greater time than I had. She took the Confederate flag off the wall and lit a match. I thought she
was going to light the small gas floor furnace. Instead, she
immolated the flag.

I was inconsolable. I considered the flag mine merely
because I had bought it and possessed it for a while. I
didn't consider that my harried but calm, brilliant and
productive mother had given me the money with which I
bought the flag. I could not have gotten the flag on my
own. I was but a boy and had no understanding or appreciation of these facts.

My mother explained that I would understand one day
and then led me out of the back room to some other
activity, probably piano practice. This only led me into
an even worse mood. I escaped it when the piano lesson
was over and never thought about flags again for a long
time.

So now the sun is my flag. I know nobody is ever going
to try to capture it. It is too strong. I know it does not
belong to me, but to all under it. Its value and meaning
are inherently benevolent. There is nothing bad about it.
The sun is my flag, not my god, as it was with some
Egyptians and Amon-Re. Such beliefs are silly.

In fact, after a certain age, one cannot believe in gods,
not and be considered an intellectual. Some people would
rather be considered intellectual than human. When you

realize how puny humans are, you can see the intellectuals' point on this matter. As intellectuals, they believe
they can figure things out. Things like, there is no God.
There is only nature, and science. When intellectuals
finally get around to believing in God, which usually happens after they get older, they have to intellectualize their
belief, as one German philosopher did.

The only reason people still remember Nietzsche is
because he was an intellectual. He is supposed to have
intellectualized that as well. As he got older, he saw the
rationale of believing—intellectually of course—because it
was safer. If he believed, and there turned out to be a
god, like the Egyptians thought, then he would be on
God's good side. It would be safer to believe, for there
wasn't that much of a difference to him between believing
and not believing. So he believed with the scientific
detachment of an intellectual.

I'm more in the camp of Amenhotep I, the Kemet-
Egyptian pharaoh, who came to the conclusion that there
is one god; he called him Aten. Amenhotep had a healthy
respect for the sun, too. Like me, he probably also
believed what he could see. Unlike me, he didn't have to
worry about television. The sun is the flag of God, not
God itself but a manifestation of God. The sun lets me
know that there is a God, although I can't say what God
calls itself. I'm not a pharaoh. I merely feel the presence
is there. I know it not because of sermons I've sat
through. I know it more because of the sun.

I cannot believe something as mighty as the sun just
happened out of a complete and total vacuum. If it had,
then that's one element of the phenomenon, a mighty orb
so immense that it lights entire worlds which were once
part of it but now circle it obediently, millions of miles
away. And the sun warms these worlds. This world has
been warmed just right so that dinosaurs and men could
safely grow on it, grow up to fight and hoist flags and
pistols and estimate the sun's life expectancy in their spare

time. Now all that is one link in an accidental chain of events. Now realize that there are billions of suns all over what men call the universe. And yet, there is no God.

I'm sorry. It makes sense to believe. It's not like the sun is just there. Every day it turns over the world and provides it with light. The sun gives people a reason to go on because it will come up tomorrow. It is the reason for life. Even if you don't believe there is a God, you know there is a sun, and you know that without it, even for mere minutes, all men would die. And after all the men are dead and their flags long decayed, if the sun decided or was ordered to return, something would come up from the water and take the place of man and go about the same business.

Everything under the sun makes too much sense for it all to have been accidental. Everything rotates, comes full circle, there are too many cycles for it not to be so. The sun dictates what we can eat, where we can eat it, where we can go and when we can go there. It shapes how we feel and what we care about.

One of the great yet simple facts of the sun has sent men into intellectual tizzies for eons. It is the simple fact that the sun causes skin color. Not intellectuals, not sperm banks, not what massa say, nothing else has anything to do with pigmentation. It is a manifestation of the power of the sun. The sun made the races of men. The closer you were to the equator, the more you were blessed by the sun.

Only men could twist this to mean that men were to be judged by races and pigmentation. Probably the most intellectual white man around these days is Stephen Jay Gould, an anthropologist and paleontologist. Those titles are there to impress the intellectuals. Actually, Mr. Gould's most impressive title is that of teacher. He seems to have thought most things through, and since he is a teacher, he should be and is magnanimous with his learnings. All in all, an admirable, memorable man.

Gould refutes quite clearly some men's desire to say that

man first came into being in Asia, not in Africa. Africa
means black men and black men are inferior. All these
things have been inferred. Stephen Jay Gould puts the
kibosh on all that with great intellectual style, writing
page after page of common sense dressed in intellectual
clothing. And even Mr. Gould admits that the saturation
bombing of racial prejudice by color—a mere, simple act
of the sun—pierced even his own high intellect. Mr.
Gould, in the May 1986 issue of *Discover* magazine:

The racist traditions of our cultures run so deep
that vestiges remain, in distant and unrecognized
form, even among those who've struggled hard to
overcome all prejudice.

I may, perhaps, underscore this point by telling a
story against myself. My friend and fellow paleontologist Bjorn Kurten wrote a fine novel, *Dance of the
Tiger*, about the contact of Neanderthal and Cro-
Magnon people in Europe some 35,000 years ago. He
depicted the "primitive" indigneous Neanderthal as
white and the "advanced," invading Cro-Magnon as
dark. This jolted me because, quite subconsciously,
I'd always pictured Neanderthals as dark and Cro-
Magnon as light. Yet I realized that Kurten's conjec-
ture is much the more reasonable—since cold-
adapted people tend to be light and Neanderthals
were a European race of Homo sapiens, while Cro-
Magnon people may have invaded from warmer cli-
mates. I then had to ask myself why I had unthink-
ingly shunned the more reasonable hypothesis. The
answer can only be vestigal racism—I had, much to
my embarrassment, equated primitive with dark and
advanced with white.

Mr. Gould had nothing to be embarrassed about,

because even intellectuals are controlled by television programs. There has never been a more apt name for what we all are forced to see on television. We are programmed. Programmed to think the way we do. Television is a flag too, but it is not as benevolent as the sun. Television can be like the Confederate flag. It can stand for power and corruption.

If you watch enough television, and most people do, you would find that the sun seems to make people act in strange ways. All the white people seem normal, but the black people seem like cardboard. All the white people are beautiful, all the black people are just around. All the white people know everything, most of the black people have to be told. The white people are portrayed in a positive light. Most of the black people are not. Intellectuals might write this off as a great cosmic accidental upheaval of nature having nothing to do with God, but I think differently.

And so, men fight and argue over what the sun has wrought, the many colors of their skins. The programming has been so effective that even among one race of people, black people, this fighting occurs. Black people have been to the four corners of the earth in a variety of situations, only one or two of which have been depicted on television. On television, you'd think the only time Africans ever got out was on slave ships. And that every shade of brown is the result of some long-past rape. Well, many shades are. But the sun had everything to do with it. In fact, it merely offers its blessing. Humans complicate it up by thinking the sun was too generous with some of them, and they think that way because of flags like the Confederate flag and television.

Complexion has become too intellectual a word for me. I prefer the word used by the old folk around where I grew up. Complected. There were light-complected people, brown-skinned people, and dark-complected people. The word *complected* makes me think of complications and afflictions, so it is a much better word for me in this context.

Complexion can confuse. Some light-complexioned people want nothing to do with dark-complexioned people. Yet you couldn't bring some light-complexioned people anything but a dark-complexioned mate. And vice versa for some dark-complexioned people. All this confusion is a result of programming. Too much television. Too many flags. Not enough sun. Yet too much sun can kill. Talk of your flag's power by comparison.

Intellectuals, once you take the bait and invite them to speak, will talk about the possibility of another great cosmic accidental upheaval of nature that has nothing to do with God. They call this one "nuclear winter." We could check it out with the dinosaurs, only no dinosaurs are left. The sun will come up tomorrow. Whether or not any of us are here to see it is another matter. Long after the Confederate flag has been forgotten, the sun will be there, shining and lording over all of whoever and whatever remains. Every new day will start with the sun. I feel blessed merely to have been one of its more fortunate subjects.

On Television

Most black people prefer watching live television. We are going to watch television anyway, whether we like it or not, so black people prefer it live. If it's already in the can, then you can bet it's *Rocky* or *Zulu* or *Zulu Dawn* or *Shaka Zulu* or the nightly news or some other form of glory for white men and debasement for black ones. One reason live television is so rare in the first place may be the fact that black people enjoy it. Why do black people enjoy live television? Because black people enjoy seeing themselves portrayed in a positive light just like everybody else who's breathing. If the televised event is live and therefore subject to reality, there is a better chance of something positive happening than if the televised event is staged.

Example: The government of South Africa sanctioned the filming of the movie entitled *Shaka Zulu*, under the corporate name of Harmony Gold. Now anything named Harmony Gold is not to be trusted in the first place. It sounds too sweet. It must be a trap. Beyond that, black people in South Africa know to reject anything offered up by the government there, or anywhere else. Black people in South Africa know better than anyone that what somebody is trying to give you, you'd better be trying to duck.

So the black and white people who disseminate background information told black people in America to be on the watch-out for this *Shaka Zulu* movie, and to be sure to ignore it. This would be for the best.

But, as often happens, the thing that is for the best turns out to be the thing that is the most difficult to do. Ignoring this film was difficult, because in America, as late as 1986, black people were so emotionally starved for film depictions which might portray black people with stiff backbones, powers of speech, a range of emotion, beauty, sensitivity, intelligence, or any other positive human qualities. There was no way black people were going to ignore all of *Shaka Zulu*, not when the alternative was reruns of "Good Times" or "The Jeffersons."

Well, black people weren't going to ignore the first three parts of the five-part *Shaka Zulu*. I think my son was typical. He watched the first three nights, when Shaka was a hero. He fell asleep in the first ten minutes on each of the last two nights, never to rouse again once the South African government's point of view began to grab Shaka by the throat and emasculate him. My son was waiting for Shaka to kiss his wife, or lift his spear, but he never did that again. The film wended its way through a morass of cheap propaganda. But, again, my son was not awake for that.

In this hemisphere, black people are accustomed to making do. When useless oil drums were left discarded on the beaches of the Caribbean, black people invented musical instruments they called steel drums. When inedible food was thrown out, slaves made Christmas dinner out of greens, yams, and back ends of animals. And the very white people who threw these items out were the ones most enhanced by the results.

Some black people watched some of *Shaka Zulu* in spite of their preference for live television. Then if they were smart, they took the good out of it and threw the rest away. My son, sleeping through the last two nights of this dogmatic treatise, was a case in point. He was five years old when he saw and slept through *Shaka Zulu*.

Black people can learn very quickly.

One thing we've learned is that if it isn't live, it isn't memorable, and it probably isn't even true.

I have a love-hate relationship with television. It is too powerful a medium to ignore. It can be and often is used to depict events which seem not to make much sense at all, and everyone says they know what garbage there is on it in general. But once something or someone is on it, that thing or person acquires a legitimacy which may or may not be deserved. I learned this with no small degree of awareness when I began appearing on television every once in a while. Not too often, mind you, but enough to get a point or two across, butcher a few others, and collect a few checks.

I first appeared on cable television, which is much less subject to control than the networks. I then appeared on network television briefly, for perhaps 120 minutes total, over a period of roughly five months. This fact seemed to take the breath away from many people, who when they saw me would say, "Hey, you're on television." I never quite knew how to react to this. I didn't know if it was an accusation or not. Then I began to realize that this was a pleasant experience for these people, everyone from strangers to those I knew well. It was as if I had suddenly become rich or a great magician. It all happened because a friend of mine had merely said, "Would you like to do it?" I said, "Yes, I think so." There was no further need for any qualifications, as the morbid and threatened looks on the faces of my coworkers in television told me once I happened to meet them.

I had always considered the people in publishing to be insecure. People in television were even more so. I took pains to tell them I had no ambition of staying on television for a protracted period, not in front of the camera, at any rate. This did not assuage them.

I tried to study my own reactions and gauge them next to the people who were on television with me. They'd been on television for years, most of them, and it showed. They could smile on cue, even if they were in the process of a heated argument. They carried small parcels of makeup. They were very sensitive to any signs of aging, disrepair, illness, or anything that might be revealed in their faces that would show that they might be human beings, affected by change. They had short attention spans and carried grudges.

They were, on the average, extremely bright and intelligent people. They were gifted at circumlocution and often used this gift. They were careful with what they said on air. Everything had to be down the middle of the road on network television, and from my perspective this was not good because that was to say everything was just fine and let's not upset the applecart, let's just get the advertisers and viewers. That is the nature of business. The most unfortunate part of television is that it is such a powerful medium which has become such a powerful business. When I was told that being on network television was not my cup of tea, I had to agree.

Being on television is now considered only slightly less important than being alive. Given that, given that television has such direct penetration into the hearts and minds of the public, a market I share with television like it or not, I have to be close to it, make peace with it, so I should know the directions in which it takes me. Many writers speak of television with disdain until they are asked to be on it or to write for it. I am not so naïve as to deny the power of the medium. But how to put a grasp on it, how to use it without it using you? This is a problem I constantly wrestle with, because those who control television also control thought processes and actions among those who are subject to the television's programming. Imagine if Adolf Hitler had controlled television. I'd rather imagine that I did.

If I controlled who could be on television, I would bar all evangelists. If they are sincere, they will write sermons and deliver them to people who want to come out. I would bar people with cute names made up for television. Then I would bar almost nothing else, of course reserving that right, much as the television executives reserve it today. So much for what I would bar. When I think of what I would allow! I would allow people who smile only when they are quite pleased, or when they think something humorous has been said or done. I would allow people who speak plainly. In fact, I would have at least one channel where people could come in off the street and for a nominal fee have sixty seconds to say anything they like. That way they could face the horrors of makeup and circumlocution and then go home and watch themselves and wince and be much less impressed with being on television. I would show all this live. Then I would wake up.

I make light of serious matters. Television has become the most powerful communicative force since the human voice and is not to be passively watched. To watch it without skepticism would be like believing everything Aunt Minnie ever told you. To watch television without thought is to be told what to think, and to be told what to think is death. Television is not out there waiting for you. It's in here waiting for you. Keep it close so you might know its plans, which I know is vague and cryptic advice at best. When the picture is not clear just turn it off.

About Personalities

Robert, Willie, David, Marion and Charles

Some women say all men are dogs. The only question is the breed. So what to make of Robert, Willie, David, Marion and Charles?

The deciders of a man's official pedigree, his potential, his perceived value and then in turn his ultimate station in life and time of departure from the mortal coil are those people—usually white—who control the prisms which color the world and fix its focus. Those who throw switches and pull triggers and beat heads are almost as victimized as those they torture. No, it is the deciders with the Great Prisms, mass media, who are to blame, and they are, in large measure, white. If they are not white, they usually decide in a manner which they hope will please the deciders who are white. Of all this you can be assured. You doubt me? Take the measure and see.

Robert Chambers is a big, strapping, slothful, blue-eyed brunet young white man who allegedly broke into apartments on the East Side of New York. He, undoubtedly, nodded sympathetically when the victims of his burglaries ground their teeth and shook their heads, waxing on about how all niggers stole—all this while filing their insurance papers—possibly without uttering a word. All well and good for the deciders and the world according to their mammoth prisms until Robert Chambers nearly twisted off the head of a girl named Jennifer Levin. She was Jewish and could be seen as white according to the deciders' reflected beams. Depending on where Jennifer was standing, depending on the light, color and spin, slant and twist and convenient irony, they would determine what she was supposed to reflect, and who and how.

I remember when Jennifer Levin was killed, not the specific date on the calendar, but the scenario. I was working for a widely circulated magazine in New York City. Widely circulated magazines are some of the very best prisms going. I was searching for ways to refract the light so the deciders would deem it acceptable, and I could live with myself at the same time. Difficult work, at best.

In a vain attempt to show me the fruitlessness of my desire to reflect and or refract light in what was deemed the proper way, the proper authorities decided to make me share an office—a very tiny office—with another writer, a man named Dan Levin. Mr. Levin happened to be the uncle of Jennifer Levin. We had spoken only as a formality on the few times we chanced to meet. Neither one of us was in the office very often. Mr. Levin was also on the outs with the proper authorities, and this was one of authority's ways of letting him know it. That is, by making him share an office with me. Two birds with one stone. I never saw Dan Levin again in the flesh after his niece was killed. But I saw him through the prism. He was anguished as the television cameras and reporters recorded him saying, "New York is a social experiment that failed."

I do not intend to cast any aspersions on Dan Levin. However, this is sometimes the way reflecters and refracters talk. When they want to say "Goddamn the niggers to hell for being near us with their uncivilized behavior," they say "It is a social experiment that failed." When they want to say "niggers," they say "crime." When they want to say "niggers," they say "welfare." When they want to say "niggers," they say "drugs." When they want to say "niggers," they say anything but "niggers," because nice and good and fair people don't say "niggers." The deciders and their well-trained and highly skilled reflecters and refracters, the rotators of the prisms, are careful with their own images, for they above all know how important these images are.

It does not matter a tittle that the niggers of their dreams had little at all to do with any of this, except on television. It took the police a few hours to find out that Robert Chambers did probably maybe kind of hold Jennifer Levin too hard. This unfortunate delay is why some people had the opportunity to speak their minds, sort of. I believed, in my own bombarded mind, that they thought, since Jennifer Levin was white and was killed in Central Park, (under the circumstances) she was killed by the wild rampaging niggers. I would wager my life that many people thought along these lines. I might win that bet.

But then the truth sort of came out and Robert Chambers was kind of exposed for the monster he maybe was. He even had a party with other girls and made them laugh by staging a mock strangulation. He eventually had to spend a little time in prison. He thought he was wronged. Meanwhile, the worms inched toward Jennifer.

I never saw or heard from Dan Levin again, which was for the best. I'm sure we would have little to share with each other, as usual. Robert Chambers was known as the "Preppie Killer." Not the murderer, the beast, the animal, but a preppie who let sexual horseplay get a little rough. What power the prisms have! I became more intent on cutting and polishing the small one I keep hidden in my pocket.

Willie Horton came under the prisms next, during the 1988 race to decide who would be President of the United States. The Democratic contender was a man of Greek ancestry, the governor of Massachusetts, Michael S. Dukakis. He seemed to be a well-meaning man, but who could tell since he had to be viewed through the distorting light? The Republican candidate was named George Bush, who also seemed to be a well-meaning man. Whether or not they were well-meaning has little to do with being elected President of the United States. The Republican candidate's backers thought this race was too close for comfort, so to ensure election, they placed a photograph of an unsmiling, unshaven, uncombed and decidedly unwhite Willie Horton under the prism, right next to Michael S. Dukakis, and just about said that Dukakis did personally let Willie Horton out of prison. Then, within fifteen minutes, without any motivation or conscience, Willie Horton went on a wild, rampaging raping spree, and Willie Horton broke into a white man's house, and Willie Horton, capable only of gross carnality and not proper love, raped the white man's wife while the man was tied up and forced to watch Willie Horton's throbbing penis. Sounds like somebody's sexual fantasy with another turn of the prism, but when talking about electing the President of the United States, it came out "Michael S. Dukakis is a nigger-lover, and niggers are crime, welfare, drugs, death and the rape of the pure woman to your left, all you white people out there, including all you potential rape victims."

I realize this may sound harsh and unwise, but I assure you I have only removed the prism from the front of it and let the raw nakedness of it show the way it affects you. This is the way you actually hear it and see it, only you don't know it, usually. It doesn't matter if you are white or black or brown or transparent. This is what you process. This is how you color. The power of the prism is very great. Needless to say in America, Michael S. Dukakis was not elected President of the United States, which might have been for the best anyway as far as I know.

The prismatic effect didn't stop when the election was over. The message was imbedded deep. Which is not to say Willie Horton didn't do some of what he was accused of doing. But in reality, which has little to do with anything anymore, Willie Horton and Willie Horton *alone* did this. Under the light of the prism, Willie was aided and abetted by me and anyone who resembles me and any white person who ever gave me the time of day by accessory. In the bizarre view through the prism, Willie Horton might have been me under an assumed name. That is the message received, imbued and acted out.

Since I knew this well, I began to tread away from a few select white people, because if by some chance I were to be caught missing my guard, I might be killed or injured or jailed for being falsely accused of killing, and then be killed in jail. Any and all of it by accident sort of. My killer would be named "The Accidental Killer" and would get a book and a movie out of it and thereby kill three birds with one stone. Since I am the first bird who would be portrayed in this act, the cooked goose, I took pains to avoid the theater. When I die I hope to have a reason.

This is where David Duke comes in. Duke was some kind of elected representative in the state of Louisiana. He was also a former Ku Klux Klansman and the founder of the National Association for the Advancement of White People, his version of the NAACP, supposedly. By this résumé, Mr. Duke isn't one of the brightest white people you'll ever meet. Either that or he doesn't care to couch his misguided, disdainful hate in verbal satin. He is no decider. He isn't qualified to be a decider. He is one of the deciders' victims. But for a Klansman, he's positively Oscar Wilde and William F. Buckley rolled into one. He sits up and talks about crime and welfare and drugs and IQ tests, so even the dumbest white people—if indeed there are any dumber than Mr. Duke—can follow him and queue up and vote their conscience.

A very unoriginal human being, this David Duke. Poisoned by the deciders in his youth, he learned his hate, and also learned how to pass off his own inadequacies on other people. If he didn't get something, it was somebody else's fault, not his. David Duke didn't leave such thinking behind in the seventh grade, like most everybody else. He had hit upon a business.

Well, of course, he had. He had hit upon a bonanza of a business, in fact. No one among the deciders did anything about David Duke because he was "sensitizing the market." No over ever treated David Duke like the petulant child he remained, and this was dangerous, because Duke was old enough and big enough to lift a gun or mail a letter bomb or light a match or encourage other people to do it for him. Yet no decider ever called him out on his own inadequacy while he was railing against what he thought was inadequate elsewhere.

I didn't consider this unusual until David Duke sat down one evening beneath the mighty prism of television. Sitting next to him was a middle-management decider and reflector named Julian Bond. Julian Bond is a black man, under certain lights, but he sat there challenging David Duke on a short level. "But didn't you say this, Mr. Duke? But didn't you do that?" Julian was trying to expose David Duke as a racist, which even made Duke smile and think, "Damn, Julian, of course I'm a racist. Don't you keep up?"

I said to myself old Julian could have exposed David Duke with just one question: "Mr. Duke, let us say you achieve this world of your dreams, a world of ninety-five percent white people of your basic racial and ethnic caste (the Michael Dukakises of the world need not apply), with about five percent of black people to do all the work for you and most of the thinking for you, and no Jewish people for you to pick on. Now suppose, by blinking your eyes, you can create this world. Do so. Now, Mr. Duke, there is no need for your National Association for the

Advancement of White People, and you would have never thought of it anyway since someone else didn't think of it first.

"So you are in this brave new world, Mr. Duke, the world of your making. Now, Mr. Duke, the question. *What would you do? What would you create? What would you make? What feats could we anticipate from you if the field were cleared and you only had to compete against your own shadow?*"

You'd have Mr. Duke there, because he is apparently short on talent. He doesn't even have the talent to be a decider, much less real artistic or technical or organizational or creative skill to occupy his time, nothing real in him but hate—which is what drove him into madness in the first place. His hate grew large and misshapen, irrorated by the microwaves and ultraviolets of the prisms. Duke wants to be considered great and be compensated and loved by a good woman who won't call him a dog to his face and will never touch another man merely because Duke is white. Period. He has done nothing worth noting except for being born and alive. I can assure him he will die, just as I will.

And what of Julian, who was not quick enough to think of such a line of questioning for the dubious Mr. Duke? Well, Julian has had problems of his own. Julian is black, according to the rules of the deciders, yet he looks mysteriously more like Duke than like Willie Horton. Julian has been an elected official and drafted a few bills, I'm sure. But he failed to ask Mr. Duke the good question, so I don't know what to make of him anymore, and I didn't have time to dwell on him long because he was abruptly removed from all the mighty prisms and replaced by Marion Barry.

Marion Barry has been for some time the mayor of Washington, D.C. For nearly a millennium, it seems, during the 1980s. And some people say he has been a good mayor, a good political organizer in his day. Some people do not say that. About like it is with all mayors, on balance. But then Marion Barry made a bad public relations gaffe. He was videotaped by law enforcement—not one of the better prisms, but certainly adequate—smoking cocaine in the Vista Hotel in Washington, in the company of a former consort, Hazel Rasheeda Moore.

Everything was understandable, if indeed not normal as such events are actually conducted, all but the part about smoking the cocaine and getting caught. Miss Moore had asked Marion over for a little party. Marion was fifty-three by then, but you know how older men and dogs are, they always think they are still faster and more nimble than any onrushing car or other vehicle, like fate. Marion said he'd be right over and no doubt he felt very much like a man as he strode into the Vista Hotel and up to what he surely thought would be yet another in his truly memorable series of assignations. Well, Rasheeda Moore, in His Honor's own words, "Set me up!" Yes, she did indeed. The Federal Bureau of Investigation now had His Honor on videotape with one thing in his hand and something else on his mind.

On the one hand, since the mayor had been given urgent warnings that he was at least suspected of frequenting such affairs with such substances in the past, he might have opened one of his eyes. On the other hand, you'd have to admit, it was a pretty good sting, the lure of sex, the company of an old friend. Some said it was racist and sure, why not? We would all be remiss if we didn't seriously doubt if such a sting would have been leveled at any elected politician other than a black mayor.

But, again, as in the case of Julian Bond, did Marion Barry just realize this once they told him he was under arrest? Was that his first inkling of racism? Was it the first time he realized that he might—heaven forbid—be the victim of it? Marion, where have you been? Don't you keep up?

On second thought, Effi Barry didn't want to know. Effi

Barry was His Honor's wife. Are you noticing a trend? It seems whenever men act up, act out, women suffer. Some positions beneath the light are even worse than my own.

Remember, the prisms had cascaded their lights on Marion Barry and Charles Stuart at the same time they shined on you and me. We were all bathed in it together. This is not to say that the light from the prism caused Charles Stuart to take his pregnant wife Carol to a childbirth class at a hospital in Boston, then escort her to their car, then shoot her point-blank in the head, thereby killing her and their unborn child. And now that Charles Stuart is himself dead, we may never know exactly why he did such a horrific deed. But Charles Stuart didn't die right away. That was the unfortunate part of it. He almost lived another lifetime.

You would think you could recognize such a monster. He would be uncombed, unshaven, unwashed and be as black as Willie Horton. Or at least Julian Bond. In fact, this was almost the description to the letter that Charles Stuart gave to the police after he had shot himself in the stomach and gotten on his car radio from the Mission Hill district, a nigger, oh-excuse-me-we're-in-reality, "inner-city" part of Boston. Charles Stuart told a police dispatcher that a black man of the above description leaped into the backseat of his car, demanded money, looked at the car phone, and thought that made Charles Stuart a cop. And it would have been just like a nigger to think Charles, a white man, resembled Magnum, P.I., the white private detective on the great prism of television. Then, Stuart explained, the man shot Carol quite neatly in the head and only then decided to shoot Charles in the stomach. (Charles resembling a cop and being much less dangerous than a pregnant woman to a twisted, drug-laced nigger mind, of course.)

And this collection of straw flew magnificently like a mammoth bird over Boston, flew without wavering over the hot emotional currents, flew through the outrage and outcry which flowed from all the prisms great and small and sent white people in Boston and across America into a mood, and made every black man on the continent who put on a black warm-up suit a possible murderer—at least an accessory after the fact. This hovering, ominous bird of prey flew over some smart white detective in Boston who figured it all out in thirty minutes and couldn't do anything but shake his head and wait for the shit to come down, because any good detective with long experience knew who the first and last suspect was in this case. Knew who did it, all but in fact. All the detectives in Boston couldn't be that dumb and naïve. Not all of them.

Meanwhile, the mayor of Boston and Governor Dukakis went to Carol Stuart's funeral. You never know. They might want to run for President someday. Outside, black men were eyed hatefully, rousted, threatened, and, for all I know, killed. Charles Stuart read a poem for his wife's funeral. He seemed very forgiving. He didn't say "nigger" once, and his friends and family marveled at how good and kind and fair he was. The police captured a few black men, hoping the killer was in their number. It would be a coup to find this nigger. Charles went to a lineup and solemnly picked one out, saying he resembled the man who had shot his wife. By that Charles meant he was a black man. This was the full description.

I will not do this haunted African-American man the disservice of mentioning his name. After all, this is a story about Charles. This black man was a small-time criminal, having long ago been victimized by the unremitting rays of the prisms. He might have been a criminal anyway, without prisms. Who knows? He hadn't killed anyone in reality. But being accused of killing someone, being almost pampered about it, being acclaimed, seeing his name in the prism as if he were some head of state, was a notice of a new order for him. It seemed almost pleasant. At least people admitted he was alive, capable of some-thing, worthy of notoriety. Maybe he did kill her. Not in reality, but beneath the prisms, where he lived, mostly. Dinner was reality. They brought dinner in jail every day, like clockwork. So maybe he did kill her.

The bird of prey soared on until Charles Stuart made a critical error. He barked. He woofed. He told. He told his brother Matthew. Charles even gave Matthew the bag with the murder weapon and the items he said the black man had stolen the night of the murder as Carol lay slumped on the front seat of the car. Charles told his brother to throw the items in the river, including the pis-tol he had used. Matthew did this, then went away. Eventually, Matthew barked as well, and the bird serenely plummeted into the Charles River knowing well it would rise like a phoenix soon.

Charles Stuart, the hero, jumped off a bridge into the Mystic River and drowned. He didn't admit to crimes in his suicide note. He just said he couldn't take being accused. He was strong enough to shoot his wife in the head, but he wasn't strong enough to be accused of doing it. The dancing prism lights can drive the weak minded violently insane.

After all this, some white people in Boston said, well, the baby Carol was carrying was a black man's. That would explain what Charles did. *That would explain it.*

Other things were said. Charles Stuart had taken out a hundred-thousand-dollar insurance policy on Carol. Charles Stuart had a girlfriend. Charles Stuart was overly ambitious. Well and good. But this business about the black baby, the new life, that was an interesting part of the fabrication. People—white people—talked about test-ing the genetic material of this poor dead fetus to see if it was composed of black genetic material or not. That would explain many things, make it all neat and nice and fair and good again, or very nearly that way. Charles had shot his wife in the head because Willie Horton had gotten her pregnant. Yes, that would explain it.

But there was blackness in him. You could say he had "a black heart," and in a sense be correct. That is the bizarre world in which we live, the utter and plain simple complexity of language. It was Charles Stuart's child that he killed. The black man who was never even there could still be blamed, even after it was sort of admitted he wasn't there. He is always there, isn't he? The eyes and the wings of the bird of prey broke the waters of the river. It shrieked with another new life.

Some men are dogs. Men have names like Robert, Willie, David, Julian, Marion and Charles. Men bathe in the light from the prisms. The deciders decide how they bathe, what is best, who should live, who will die.

If it weren't for the small realities like dinnertime, we would all be doomed. We all are doomed anyway. Men are dogs, women decree, and women are the only ones who can give life in reality. Women are the true deciders. That is what makes men so desperate. Only women can bestow life, in reality. They did us the favor once, and look what was done with it. That is why women say most men are dogs. Because Robert, Willie, David, Julian, Marion and Charles all lived with or around women at one time or another. Women bore them, fed them, supported them, were hurt and killed and compromised by them. The prisms want to convince us it is only black men who are guilty of this treason. Only black men have no ability to give life, just to take it.

Smart, experienced women know all men are to be feared and watched and controlled. I'd love to see them get their hands on the big prisms for a little while, for my own sake as well as theirs. At least they might spread the blame around. Meanwhile I keep a steady eye around me to avoid the bird of prey's wide shadow while I unconsciously bathe in the pelting, refracted rays. I cannot avoid the light. So I grimly twist my own prism in my own small corner, watch the thin light of my making and feel a most private fascination. This is the only life I can give or create. This is the only time I am not a mad dog by association if nothing else. This is why I stay alone.

Crossover and Michael Jackson

I cannot understand why black people become upset with Michael Jackson and accuse him of "crossover." I can't see why anyone would mind. Michael is just following the crowd.

It's like I used to hear in the words of that old Negro spiritual, which I first sang out of a songbook written, published and distributed by non-Negroes: *De-e-eep river, I want to cross over Jordan into campground.* I'm sure Michael knows a meaningful lyric when he hears it. You've got to say that for him. Those aren't stringy locks atop his head. To Michael, those locks are dollar bills. And that nose. Michael paid good money for that nose. Why? Because soon his nose would pay for itself, and then some. That isn't Michael's nose. That's his campground.

People search through life for a philosophy. Since we are in America, it follows that a good philosophy would have economic principles. Michael Jackson crosses over, just like that old Negro spiritual says, so he can get paid. Life in America is based on getting paid, as you know if you've ever been or know anyone who has ever been to New York City.

Sometimes being a good citizen, paying taxes and doing

a good job of whatever you do for a living doesn't necessarily mean you'll get paid, especially if you're related by either blood or appearance to the subjects of old Negro spirituals. We all have to get paid, one way or another, or we end up sleeping outdoors, starved or dead.

Michael Jackson wanted to get paid and then some, so he crossed over and then some. That's how you get paid a lot in America if you are black. You cross over and then some. Black musicians have crossed over into pop and been pilloried for it by black people. White pop musicians cross over into jazz, or rap, or wherever they can navigate the stream, but nobody pillories them, and even if somebody does, as long as that somebody isn't the somebody who is signing the checks, so what?

Only blacks are made to feel restricted from crossing over. They shouldn't have crossed over from the thoughtful nuances of jazz to the pop charts. They "sold out." Now, accusing someone of selling out is a serious charge, not to be thrown about or taken lightly. The phrase *selling out* conjures up all kinds of images of people selling people, and their souls as well. But this kind of selling out has nothing to do with souls. This has to do with the almighty pocketbook first. Only then does it have to do with souls. Let's keep the musicians in the focus the better to keep them off balance. Don't apply the selling-out test to me, or you, or things might become unmanageable. Let's keep it on the musicians, whose only answer is more music and therefore open to interpretation.

For the black musicians accused of crossing over, the simple equation said that, somehow, being on pop charts pays better. The musicians did the smart thing in a business sense, which doesn't at all mean they were prohibited from playing music on their own time, does it? Michael, however, is more or less stuck with circumstances.

Some of the black people who complain about Michael Jackson and other musicians, actors and stars crossing over do a pretty good job of crossing over themselves, and they aren't getting paid nearly as well. We cross over at work if we happen to go to work at Fortune 500 companies. We cross over when we buy vapid pop albums, or when we buy songbooks of Negro spirituals published by non-Negro people or when we criticize a black filmmaker like Spike Lee for hitting too close to home, while spending good money to go and see how white filmmakers will ignore us next.

I had a bet with the person who helped me sell these essays. I said the buyer would be a black publisher. He disagreed. I lost.

So, in the end, we all cross over to some extent, which is good for the circulation—or better be. Michael Jackson isn't blind or dumb, even if he doesn't look the same as he did once. If black people bought the jazz albums, or bought black-owned or produced goods and services, then there wouldn't be as much fun and profit in crossover. Possibly, Michael Jackson would not now resemble pottery from the Ming Dynasty. Don't blame Michael for crossing over. Blame yourself for showing him that it was the thing to do. It's always best when you can get paid and be yourself at the same time. It's more sane. One day, black people might get together and try it.

Me and Bruce and
Dan Jenkins

Let me say right off the top that Dan Jenkins doesn't know me from the mayor of Tuskegee and is probably better off. But people have been throwing me up to Dan Jenkins for a long time, so I am forced to do something about it.

Dan Jenkins is a white man, a sportswriter by trade who worked at newspapers, then at *Sports Illustrated*, then beyond. I am a black man, a sportswriter by trade who worked at newspapers, then at *Sports Illustrated*. From there, the similarities between us split, headed off in different directions, sped up and kept going to opposite ends of the universe, then on out to where even Carl Sagan and the mojo lady couldn't find them.

Still, some people threw me up to Jenkins. This was bad for him and bad for me, which, I suppose, was the intention all along. When people started this, Jenkins must have been in his fifties, a white-haired native of Texas, an expert on golf, the author of best-sellers about pro football, a humorist who could be thrown up to the best of them, and a writer who had seen and undoubtedly cashed large checks from Hollywood banks. A regular in The

Show. I, on the other hand, was breathing. You can imagine my surprise when my boss at *Sports Illustrated* got
mad one day and said:

"He's trying to be like Dan Jenkins!"

I got the impression it wasn't meant as a compliment.

When I had arrived at *Sports Illustrated*, the officers
there had told me to make myself comfortable in Dan
Jenkins's office. He was hardly ever around, they said.
Now how was I supposed to make myself comfortable in
the office of a guy who had written best-sellers about pro
football and seen and cashed checks from Hollywood
banks? I loved to rag, ignore and otherwise harass pompous people who had nothing to back up their pomposity.
But people who had the talent to be pompous, well, they
were the only real royalty in this life. Dan Jenkins's favorite song might have been "Cotton-Eye Joe," but he had
talent. I wasn't even in the same league with Dan Jenkins.
But I had twenty years to get there. Yet the bosses had put
me in his office right away. Maybe they were trying to
insult him or just tell him something. Me, too.

Well, time went by and I briefly got my own office, but
by then I was hardly ever around so they gave mine away
too. As for Dan Jenkins, he eventually left *Sports Illustrated* in a huff, probably having never gotten over
finding out what they did with his office when he wasn't
around. By then he had over 250 bylined stories in the
bank, not to mention twenty-three years, so he could
leave and say Dan Jenkins had been there and still get
early retirement.

"You're trying to be like Dan Jenkins!"

You can see how this seemed wrong-headed to me. I
had had three or four bylines. I had maybe six months on
the job. A check from a Hollywood bank could hit me in
the forehead and I'd swear it was just a headache. Best-
sellers were books I didn't buy and criticized, but never
wrote. I was from the Mississippi Delta country, by way
of Chicago, by way of California. I didn't have white

hair. So why was I thrown up to Dan Jenkins? Why didn't they throw me up to, say, Wendell Smith? You never even heard of Wendell Smith? Perfect.

But no, it was Dan Jenkins for me. Since that time, I have tried to throw Dan Jenkins back. I have not succeeded. I ended up with around two hundred plus bylines at *Sports Illustrated*. Where Jenkins got the strength for those last fifty or so, I'll never know. I once had a cup of coffee and a sinker near a Hollywood bank. I will write a book about pro football one day. It will sell well around my house. I have developed a family of thirty-nine white hairs. They are separated. I have a friend I can call before six in the evening who knows a great deal about golf. As a humorist, you can throw me up there with your dentist. So now, officially, I am severing my unofficial ties to Dan Jenkins. I am not trying to be like him anymore, which is absolutely, irrevocably final and all very good news to Jenkins, I'm sure.

No, I'm not trying to be like Dan Jenkins. So there.

One of my friends and former coworkers is a white man named Bruce Jenkins. I think Bruce Jenkins was born with a baseball in his crib. He was obsessed with the game. He probably still is. We used to travel together on the baseball beat, when he was working with the *San Francisco Chronicle* and I was working with the *Oakland Tribune*. No one ever threw Jenkins up to me and no one that I knew of ever threw me up to Jenkins. If they had, we both probably would have known better. We got along well. We had similar tastes. Once the baseball All-Star game was held in Oakland, and Jenkins and I sat in the press box and clicked off our all-time National League All-Star teams. Catcher Johnny Bench. Second base Joe Morgan. Shortstop Ozzie Smith. Third base Mike Schmidt. Left field Aaron. Center field Mays. Right field Clemente. First base Stan Musial, because he had to play somewhere with that bat. Jenkins and I picked the same

All-Star team, and about ten minutes apart, without consulting. We had similar tastes in baseball matters.

We both were about thirty-five years old at the time. A
younger man was sitting with us. He thought he was
obsessed with baseball. He didn't know how far he'd have
to go to top Jenkins in that department. After we listed
our teams, the younger man said incredulously, "Rogers
Hornsby isn't at second base on your team?" Now, Rogers
Hornsby had played before my and Jenkins's time, long
before the young man's time. We had something like a
dozen years on the kid. I guess he felt by picking
Hornsby, he showed he had done his research on things
like career batting average and whatnot. But Jenkins and
I had *seen* Joe Morgan hit some of the home runs which
had given him more home runs than any second baseman
who ever lived. And little Joe could steal a base, too. Jenkins and I knew what we were doing. That I knew from
history that Rogers Hornsby was racist to the core was a
happy coincidence. Why, I'd have had Jackie Robinson on
my team way before I would have had this guy. Jenkins
sends me a card from time to time from Hawaii or Malibu
or wherever the hell he is now.

Bruce, not Dan.

I don't expect one from Dan.

What the AIDS Doctor Says

One of the most beautiful sights in nature is the shape of a well-stocked pair of blue jeans hugging the sloping curve of two female legs, all firmly balanced on the base of a fine pair of ankles. I do not need excuses for my taste. I am a male hominid, and certain blue jeans make me glad of it. I was given the gifts of twenty-fifteen vision and a full appreciation of what God hath wrought in women. Jeans only accentuate.

Watching blue jeans was once my favorite sport. But that beautiful sight and whatever topped it has been distorted by AIDS. AIDS is a plague called Acquired Immune Deficiency Syndrome. It is passed through blood or by sexual contact. AIDS will leave you quite dead, there is no known cure, and Surgeon General C. Everett Koop said no cure is likely. A vaccine might come, one day. But no cure.

I ask myself, could the forces of nature be so cruel? I do not know the answer. I am not a physician. Even if I were a physician, I might not know the answer, but I would feel worse about it then because if I were a physician, knowing everything would be my line of work. I am only curious.

Supposedly, AIDS is most likely to be passed through a homosexual encounter. I'm not too worried about such encounters, other than the thought which is always with a black man that says, *You know, bro, you can be slammed in jail just for the hell of it much more quickly than the next man.* If I did happen to visit jail for a while, either through fault of my own or not, I would not have much choice in terms of sexual proclivity. I could either be raped, or kill somebody and be in jail for the rest of my life to prevent being raped. I could get AIDS either way.

AIDS can also be passed through blood transfusions, say the doctors. I know a man who had an ulcer. He went to the hospital and needed a blood transfusion. The good and efficient people at the hospital made him sign a waiver which proclaimed that he couldn't sue if he somehow got AIDS from the transfused blood. The man signed the proclamation with a shaky hand. So now, I'm to understand, I can't even have an accident. If I do, I'll catch AIDS. There will be no need for me to sign the proclamation. If I'm about to die, I think that an island in the Caribbean would be preferable to a stuffy court-room.

So now I try and avoid sharp objects and hospitals, because if I do receive blood and am soon dying from the one remaining contaminated supply in all the United States, I am sure some lawyer will talk me out of the Caribbean. All this could be circumvented by not needing blood. But how does one prepare for that? By locking one-self in the bathroom and using depilatories only?

Just to make us sleep better, the doctors have also informed us there is a chance for AIDS to be passed through heterosexual contact, in which case I am a goner for sure. I like my sexual hetero. Always have. White peo-ple think black people like sex. And white people are right about this, too, at least in my case, and frankly, I'm not the least bit apologetic about it. And I see nothing wrong with being impressed by a pair of well-stocked blue jeans hugging the long slow slope firmly planted on the base of a perfect pair of ankles. Let others admire Trump Tower or a Jackson Pollock. Men created those sights. There is no sight a man can create which can equal the sight of a woman. No news there.

But now legs in jeans have lost their timeless allure. Things have begun to sag in my mind. Ankles are thicker. I am saddened because AIDS has done this to me. Someone has defecated on my pyramids, drawn buckteeth on my Mona Lisa, made off with my classic bust of the beauteous Nefertiti.

For some people the issue is decidedly more serious.

So it was not purely out of selfishness that I sought answers. I could not search as a doctor would. I just read what I could find. And there, in the August 9, 1987, edition of *The Washington Post Magazine*, was an article by David Remnick. Remnick's subject in this issue was Dr. Robert Gallo, the scientist who discovered the AIDS virus, and who now studied it in Building Thirty-Seven in his lab in Bethesda, Maryland.

Dr. Gallo was going through a tough time. He said he had found the AIDS virus, but apparently some critics had accused him of inventing it. They were called "Eastern Bloc critics" by David Remnick, which I suppose meant they weren't to be trusted as much as Western Bloc critics. I don't trust critics of any bloc, so I went along too.

Apparently, Dr. Gallo was disputed in his claim of being the scientist who discovered the AIDS virus by a French scientist, Luc Montagnier. David Remnick didn't call him Dr. Luc Montagnier, which served to make me pull for Luc in this matter. Since he had not been credited as a doctor, then it would have been harder for him to find the AIDS virus, I assumed. Maybe he was just a writer who liked blue jeans and had gone further out of his way to find out why he couldn't like them anymore.

On the other hand, I wondered why either one of them would want to take credit for such a discovery. It's the kind of information that I would have mailed to a newspaper in an envelope with no signature and no return address. But I suppose credit is credit and everybody wants some. I pressed on to learn more.

Dr. Gallo was a thinker and Remnick was right there with him, introducing biographical matter unobtrusively.

. . . Gallo began reading widely in chemistry and the history of medicine. He started with books like Paul De Kruif's *Microbe Hunters*, a hyperbolic history of Pasteur and the other pioneers of microbiology . . . soon Gallo was impressed in the rudiments of chemistry, valences and specific gravities, the inert gases and Avogadro's Law . . . a summa cum laude graduate of Providence College, star of his class at Thomas Jefferson Medical College in Philadelphia . . .

I was impressed with this background. Indeed, this was why Remnick had noted it, to impress the reader. I pressed on, sure that soon Remnick would let Dr. Gallo take over in the story and tell me something I could really use.

The subject turns to Africa, where AIDS is most prevalent and probably began. Gallo and nearly all others in the field believe the virus began around the rural areas near Lake Victoria. The virus probably passed from African green monkeys into man when hunters ate the animals or, less likely, when monkeys bit their human predators. "Who really knows," Gallo says blithely. "Maybe there's some ritual with monkey blood—who knows? They do a lot of funny things in Africa, like when they make their lower lip stick out or when they put things through their noses." According to Gallo, Belgian missionaries reported illnesses resembling AIDS as many as 25 years ago, but those reports soon passed. Tribes were more isolated from one another then, and such a disease was unlikely to go far. The virus began its spread with the change in African demographics and sexual habits. "Tribes began to be less isolated," Gallo says. "There was more social and sexual contacts between tribes, and people began moving more to the cities. There's been a rise in prostitution and promiscuity. The infection rate in places like Zaire and Kenya is astronomical . . . The ancient Romans had a saying: 'Anything new . . . Africa . . .'"

So much for education.

I marveled at the gall of Dr. Gallo. The man was even named for it. Obviously, Luc Montagnier had discovered the virus. If what Dr. Gallo was saying was the result of long scientific research, then someone should give me the key to Building Thirty-Seven and my own laboratory and let's see what I can do. It was interesting how Dr. Gallo gave the credit for finding the virus to himself, but the credit for founding the disease to Africans with things through their noses and their lips stuck out and to green monkeys. And not just Africans. Haiti was supposedly a hotbed of the killer virus, too. So it was black people in general.

I don't need a laboratory to smell sour milk and bad eggs. The lines about tribes intermingling and people moving from the country to the city and a little prostitution on the side described every modern civilization on earth. So how come AIDS started in Africa and not, say, Japan?

Ah yes, the dreaded green monkey. The only time I've heard of people eating monkeys was in a Steven Spielberg movie. Even if these Africans had eaten monkeys—

although we only have Dr. Gallo's word to go on here—green monkey meat just doesn't figure to metastacize into a killer disease which is sexually transmitted. Not to me. I guess I'd have to go the Thomas Jefferson Medical College to understand.

Now I can have no opinion on this matter because I am not a physician and therefore I am ridiculous. But this is what I've heard. I've heard that a certain percentage of the homosexual community in New York and elsewhere in the United States used the island of Haiti and prepubescent, virginal boys there in a private bacchanal that would have put Caligula to shame.

I have heard syphilis went untreated in a community of black people in central Alabama, near Tuskegee, during the 1940s. This inaction was federally approved, and implemented by scientists and physicians. I have heard people say it's awfully strange that a disease would turn out to be so intractably political, picking out the homosexuals and a disproportionately high number of black people as victims.

I wonder why, after thousands of years of making love any way they wanted and eating fresh food and getting their exercise and living next door to green monkeys, black people around Lake Victoria would spring forth with a disease to scour love from humanity? One place man first walked was around Lake Victoria. Why are these people given credit for death and not life?

Maybe it's not for me to know. After all, I am not a physician, much less an all-powerful genetic engineer. I'm just a middle-aged black American male who knows a great pair of blue jeans when he sees them filled up. I can only applaud David Remnick for doing a thorough job of revealing what the AIDS doctor says. I can only trust Dr. Gallo about as far as I can throw the Trump Tower. I can only hope some African shaman from around Lake Victoria and straight out of Dr. Gallo's nightmare of lips and noses and rituals and rites and genetics and atrocities comes along with a potion that will stop AIDS and bring back my blue jeans to me.

It's like the man said: Anything new . . .

When Black People Lose Hope

On December 8, 1987, David Burke, thirty-five, a long-time employee of the USAir company, smuggled a .44 caliber magnum handgun with an eight-inch barrel aboard Pacific Southwest Airlines flight 1771, originating in Los Angeles and destined for San Francisco. Burke brought the plane down into a hillside near Templeton, California, north of Big Sur. In all, forty-three people were killed. One person, Raymond F. Thomson, Burke's former boss, was probably dead before the plane crashed, shot in his seat. Burke then went forward to the cockpit, where it is said he emptied the revolver. The plane plunged twenty-two thousand feet like a kite without a tail and crashed into matchsticks, along with the whys and hows. Only the dead had the horrible answers to what occurred during this brief hell above earth. Burke's vendetta was complete.

After some facts were in, black people realized that this was not a random act. A horrible act, to be sure, and the last act of a desperate man. But it didn't seem to be impetuous. Impetuous is a pie in the face. This was loss of hope. Black people seemed to understand the rage and the frustration behind the act, if not the act itself. When does rage boil over into an abstraction, a suicidal madness?

A friend of mine said, "It seems strange to me. Usually a brother will slip into drugs or religion or petty crime behind the kind of crap this guy went through. But mass murder? Nah. The bottom line to a brother is survival. A brother knows how to *act*. We've been acting all our lives, to survive."

A woman relative of mine said to me, "We all want to kill the boss sometimes, no matter who or where or what color we are. Some people have even done it. I just can't understand why he took those other people with them. I understand the feeling, but not the deed."

David Burke had been born in London of Jamaican heritage. He was gifted, apparently, with a concrete work ethic and a facility with money. He moved to Rochester, New York, with his parents when he was a boy, and at the age of twenty-one took an entry-level job with USAir, planning to work his way up the corporate ladder.

He made several small but profitable real estate investments over the next ten years, as well as the odd auto repair for pay. He fathered four to seven (the reports were conflicting) children over that time. In his thirteenth year with USAir, he was transferred from Rochester to Los Angeles International Airport. Apparently this move was accepted by Burke since it placed him near his co-worker and fiancée, who had also been transferred to LAX, the Los Angeles International Airport.

Once in California, David Burke found himself caught up in the times. He was passed over for promotion despite his diligence on the job. He was, in fact, demoted, to ticket agent. This was the first demotion he had ever suffered at USAir, and the demotion did not rest easily on the minds of his fiancée and family. Apparently, Burke took it hard himself. He took it personally, where usually black people take these kinds of events collectively. It *was* personal, but collectively. Probably due to naïveté, Lynch considered it racism true enough, but racism directed at *him* because of *his* blackness. This is a fairly common misperception among Caribbean immigrants to America. There is not an obvious caste system here, so they somehow feel by dint of hard work they will not be like black Americans who were born and raised here. They then see the racism they still end up suffering as a personal affront. They never expect to be treated this way in America; that kind of behavior is not America, so it must be them.

He had found himself under the command of Raymond F. Thomson. Burke was fired by Thomson toward the end of 1987, apparently because the former had taken sixty-nine dollars of the proceeds from in-flight liquor sales. But black people would know that this was merely the *way* he was fired, not why he was fired.

The black people that I talked to who had worked for airline companies scoffed at the notion. It seems that the sacred in-flight liquor sales money is no more than petty cash for the stewardesses. Nobody makes a big deal out of it. It isn't even listed among the incoming assets on balance sheets of some airlines. Liquor is thrown at the first-class passengers without letup, and there is no great accounting for this. Yet a fourteen-year employee is fired for taking sixty-nine dollars from this sacred account.

Lynch told his parents that he had been suspended. They had recently given him thirty thousand dollars of their own money to invest for them. Burke had planned on bringing three of his children to California for Christmas, but having been fired from the airline company, he would have to pay full rates. He didn't tell his family back in Rochester that he had been fired. Early in the afternoon of December 8, Burke made a final plea to Thomson. It went unheeded.

So he boarded the plane and wrote a note to Thomson, who was also aboard, heading home to northern California, to Marin County, to Tiburon. Reportedly, the note said, "Hello, Ray. It's sort of ironical that we end up like this. I asked for leniency for family. Well, I got none and you'll get none." Apparently not. Everybody died.

The tragedy aside, black people understood the scenario, especially in the age of Reagan, the age of societal givebacks and corporate lynchings, economically speaking. Black people recognized that these happened as a matter of course in the 1980s, and it was best to be prepared for them. The only stable and secure job was one where you worked for yourself. There was no such thing as a loyal company. You could be loyal to the company, in fact better be loyal to the company, but with no recompense guaranteed, or even considered owed. A smart black person didn't even count on it.

David Burke had worked at USAir for fourteen years, and apparently worked well and was law-abiding. Yet he was still passed over for promotion and in fact demoted. Then he was fired for "stealing" sixty-nine dollars in inflight liquor receipts. And because he was fired this way, fourteen years of service went down the drain. All the accrued benefits that Burke was supposed to have gotten were reabsorbed by the company, and any good company man knew in his heart that Raymond Thomson had done a good job. As for Burke, it would be a lesson, a hard lesson no doubt, but a lesson. And that was supposed to be that. It happens all the time.

Only Burke lost control and took forty-four lives including his own just so Thomson wouldn't fire anybody else.

After the tragedy, the news services and newspapers did their best to color the tragedy their own way. Burke's name was mentioned as having been part of drug probes in Rochester. Never mind that he never had been charged. Black people know they haven't lived unless their name has been associated with one probe or another. Burke had been "suspected." But black people in America always are suspected, especially if they are doing things well and doing them by the book. David Burke's brother had died of a heroin overdose. Maybe Burke had helped him out with his habit, but there was no evidence that Burke had ever done drugs or sold drugs. Yet in the media the drug stain was there.

There was the matter of his seven "out-of-wedlock" children. Never mind that the fine playwright Sam Shepard had two out-of-wedlock children, and his lover, Jessica Lange, had three. They were artists. It was David Burke who had the bastard children, which was supposed to say something about him between the lines, in code, even though he took care of his offspring. Also, his girlfriend had tried to distance herself from Burke. At thirty-five, he had decided this was the woman he wanted to settle down with, but she was not so sure anymore. His reaction was portrayed as crazy, even though we all, black, white and in between, go a little crazy when the person we thought we were going to spend our lives with decides that it's not that hot of an idea. David Burke cut up some of his girlfriend's clothes and called her and hung up on her. This was proof of the "dark side" of his nature.

In fact, the only time the "bad" side of Burke's nature showed up was when he brought the plane down. There was nothing in his conduct prior to that to indicate he would lose control.

Meanwhile, Thomson, who certainly was victimized in the end, was just as certainly portrayed that way. He lived in Marin County, and had turned down several attractive job offers in other cities because he didn't want to leave Marin County, a largely white enclave north of San Francisco.

He refused to give a fourteen-year employee a second chance, any consideration—in fact, it appeared he had to be looking hard for a reason to terminate Burke, if it took a sixty-nine-dollar theft of in-flight liquor sales to get the job done. Anything would have been better than that. But he took what he could get. Stealing would stand up, even though it could be argued that he stole a lot more money than that from Burke by passing him over for promotion.

This was a sad story of American corporate life, and of death, which knows no company affiliation. I supposed the way white people understand Pik Botha, black people understood the arithmetic, if not the act. Black people are not known for their mass murdering panache, but in the late eighties, strange things had been happening.

In 1985, a black woman, for no apparent reason, had driven her car onto a sidewalk in Reno, Nevada, killing a number of people. In 1986, a black man named Larry Davis in New York City had fired upon policemen who came to "arrest" him in connection with criminal activity, and was a fugitive at large for days after his escape. Davis was suspected of murdering four drug dealers. His trial began in late 1987, precisely when four manslaughter convictions and one acquittal came in for a group of white youths involved in a racial incident in Howard Beach, Queens, New York, in which a black man had been killed by a moving car.

Then, near Christmas, several mass killings occurred, from Londonderry, New Hampshire, to Algona, Iowa. One white man, Ronald Gene Simmons, Sr., of Russellville, Arkansas, killed sixteen people, fourteen of them within his own family.

On December 14, 1987, Corporal Robert W. Raimond, twenty-seven, a white member of the Prince Georges County police force, shot and killed Officer James L. Gordon while Gordon stood in his own home. Raimond was ostensibly investigating a burglary, saw Gordon, and shot and killed him with no thought of just waiting outside and calling for backup. Again, this horrified black people, but in a cold way.

Black people expected it somehow. Somehow, Burke's story was most chilling of all because he didn't seem to be mentally ill. He wasn't sick. He wasn't some redneck given a gun, a badge and a license to kill. David Burke was only a black man who felt without hope.

Who Are the Black Leaders?

After reading many newspapers and watching television, I have been left with the conclusion that the most highly recognized black leaders in America are Jesse Jackson, Louis Farrakhan and Meadowlark Lemon. Luckily this is not an inescapable fact. Nothing against any of them. God bless them all. I know Mr. Jackson and Mr. Farrakhan are black leaders because there are always a lot of black people standing around them nodding their heads while Jesse and Louis speak. Mr. Lemon is a leader *as far as white people are concerned:* an approximation of leadership, kind of like an ambassador to white people. Jesse the Preacher, Louis the Militant and Meadowlark the Basketball Player. Everything nice, neat, easy.

Black people are not usually at liberty to choose our own ambassadors. So Meadowlark and Pearl Bailey made their way to the front of potential ambassadors and white people embraced them, just like Jesse and Louis, only in a different way. Jesse, Louis, Meadowlark and Pearl have brought joy and pain to many people. But then so have you and I. They just brought more of both to more people. But they are no more leaders than any of us are. They're just more famous.

Jesse, Louis, and Meadowlark are leaders true enough, as was the late Pearl Bailey, but they work part-time at the job. Wherever a leader goes, other people follow. This ..is not true of these four. Black people will follow them, but not anywhere.

Actually there are around a million black leaders. You just can't find them in the Yellow Pages under **B.** or **L.**

I base this assumption on a lifetime of rigorous research, and not on the guest list for the White House state dinner honoring Mikhail Gorbachev in December of 1987. Meadowlark Lemon and Pearl Bailey were on that list. I don't know if this was Raisa's or Nancy's list, but the black people invited were Meadowlark and Pearl. This gave me a feeling of disquiet, and I didn't know why, particularly. I had thought a Reginald Lewis, the Wall Street lawyer, or a Barbara Jordan type would be on the guest list, but I suppose economics and political thought were not to be themes around this state dinner. I'm sure basketball came up often.

Once there were a handful of visible black leaders. Serious men and women, not comfortable stereotypes. The only problem was that these serious men and women were ignored, conspired against, or killed. That is the number one problem with being a black leader in America. If you are good at it, then you stand to be killed. This is not speculation by any means. This has been the proven course of events and goes along with the mission, especially if you are serious.

I learned this fact when I was very young.

At that time, the white leader I had been most impressed with in American history was Thomas Jefferson, undoubtedly a brilliant man, the framer of the Constitution. If Thomas Jefferson had been immortal and subject to reasonable discourse, then it is quite likely that all Americans could have one leader, and black people wouldn't necessarily need a separate category for our leaders. A little-known black historian named J. A. Rogers attempted to portray Jefferson as a man of some African ancestry. I don't know. I would tend to doubt it. But I know what he liked. Thomas Jefferson had a consort, a sister named Sally Hemmings, a woman of color who bore him at least three children. This may be one reason why these days you don't hear of many white people named Jefferson.

By my sixteenth year, my heroes were W. E. B. Du Bois, Paul Robeson and Ida B. Wells. There were things about the fates of my group of leaders that saddened me, even with all their great accomplishments. Du Bois had gone to some of the great universities of the world—and ended up moving to Ghana in frustration. Robeson had been a Renaissance man of the first rank, an Ivy Leaguer like Du Bois, All-American athlete, dramatic star, world-class baritone—and he ended up having to go to Europe and Russia to be appreciated. Ida B. Wells was a journalist, a found of newspapers, the dogged researcher and recorder of lynchings, and was never credited as one of the great journalists of American history. Their flaws could not be helped. They led.

The two greatest black leaders of my youth were undoubtedly Martin Luther King, Jr., and Malcolm X. I heard many pleasant sounds in my youth. The sawing songs of crickets in the dusks of summer. The majestic thunderstorms inside whose grandeur I stood transfixed. The soft, reflective whistling of old people sitting on their front porches while youth flew by in front of them. The excitement of cheering. But the sounds that made the greatest impact on me were the sounds of gunshots I did not hear.

Martin Luther King, Jr., had been shot in the neck and killed at the Lorraine Motel, a few miles from where I sat at home on Saratoga Avenue in Memphis, two springs before I graduated from high school. The Lorraine Motel was a black-owned establishment, made famous by its radio commercials: "Sweet Lorraine, Sweet Lorraine," the little jingle went. My cousin was home from the Navy. He flooded into tears at the horrible news, which, incidentally, came not first from the television, but by disbelieving word of mouth. "They didn't have to shoot the man," my cousin said. I didn't need an IQ test to figure out who "they" were.

The people who were responsible for me, my leaders, would not let me out of the house. Here had been the Reverend Martin Luther King, Jr., with all the degrees and honors and encomiums and respect any one man could claim to possess without repeating himself. Here was a genuinely sincere man. And still he had been shot down for espousing a philosophy of nonviolent social change. He pounded on for equality on the strict condition of nonviolent means to that end. Even such a pure rhetoric had been too imposing for another man or group of men to accept. So he was killed. He led too well.

King had lived and died with what I consider the greatest freedom of all—the means and the ability to speak his mind. This freedom emanated from his being a minister, a preacher, more so than from his being a child of Jefferson's Constitution or a Nobel Peace Prize winner. It had been ministers who were the black men who had the freedom to speak and the pulpit to speak from and therefore be representatives of the so-called black communities like the one I grew up in, the communities where people of all shades and hues lived under the umbrella of their blackness, which kept us out of the sun, but also kept us out of the rain.

Both of my grandfathers had been Methodist ministers. I wonder if that was because they had been "called" or because they had been smart. In their times, the 1930s and 1940s, it was a question of being a railroad porter or a chauffeur or tending gardens. Those were the good jobs in the private sector. If you had a father who was a doctor and you were lighter than a paper sack, then you might become a doctor. You might move north to Industrial Heaven and get a factory job. Or you could go to the armed services. Or you could preach. Those were the options for my grandfathers.

When I was a teenager, my grandmother would often ask me, "Son, have you been called?" She meant to know if and when I would be called to preach the gospel. I wonder if she asked me out of her hopes or her fears. She probably knew I talked too much to be secure in the context where she had always thought of herself and her men as secure, and the King and all the other assassinations merely brought this home more clearly to her in her later years.

I always told her I had not been called, but when I was called, I would be sure to let her know. I was called to be a writer, and it so happened or was destined that I was fortunate to come along at a place in a time of history when my calling was my fate. With such blind luck I had been born.

"Son, have you been called?"

"No'm. Not just yet. I like to write, though."

"Take my advice. Write sermons."

I didn't feel the reverberations from another set of gunshots until years after they occurred—when, shockingly, a girl in my homeroom delivered a baby during the summer after our junior year. She named her baby Malcolm. I asked her, why that name? She said, "Because of Malcolm X." I immediately began to try and find out who this Malcolm X was, since I had never seen him on television or read about him in the newspapers, and here people were naming their babies after him. I found out, and was impressed.

Malcolm X's philosophy was self-determination. Some people, black and white, believe until this day that Malcolm X's philosophy was violence. And Malcolm led me to believe those people can think whatever they want—as long as they don't push me into the gutter or lynch me or castrate me or stop me from implementing my ideas. Coming to know Malcolm's rhetorical genius, I know he said this in reply: "There's only one way to be free. It's not something that someone gives you. It's something that you take. We will not be nonviolent with those who are not nonviolent with us."

Malcolm X never affirmed the use of violence, unless it was in the context of self-defense. I felt all people, especially my people of color, sorely needed that right.

I found a record album of excerpts of Malcolm X's speeches, the autobiography which he had told in fine detail to Alex Haley, and a book from my mother's vast collection, entitled *Who Speaks for the Negro?* by Robert Penn Warren. I didn't care for the title of that book only because I didn't feel any black leader spoke for me, necessarily. I wanted to be my own captain and judge my own positions. I didn't feel anyone needed to speak for me. Of course, I was still a child in many ways, but I felt I could speak for myself and get into trouble on my own. I read Robert Penn Warren's book, and the voices of the Whitney Youngs, Bayard Rustins, James Farmers. Robert Penn Warren took pains not to be patronizing, but how could he not be? But when he got around to Malcolm X, the book deepened dramatically.

From this autobiography, I gathered the central fact from his days as a schoolboy was when he was told by a white counselor—in Michigan, no less—that Malcolm couldn't become what he wanted to become, a lawyer, and that he should instead look into carpentry, a good honest trade. This was not a matter of grades or IQ tests. Malcolm Little was very bright and often proved it. But he was black. Eventually, Malcolm X would find his courtroom, where he could flash brilliantly as an orator and image maker. In reading of his personal triumph, I was ecstatic for him.

Robert Penn Warren, a writer, eventually the poet laureate, a Southern white man, had been honest enough to record his reaction, which was different from mine:

> But Malcolm X has, in fact, never had any associa-
> tion with actual violence on behalf of the Negro
> cause. He has always, by happy accident or clever
> design, been somewhere else.

As I saw it, Malcolm was not advocating violence. He
was merely stating a fact: I will defend myself. You
should, too. But such a simple philosophy was outlandish
at the time. Outlandish to older black people, who knew
they could be dragged off to jail or beaten on a whim or
even killed. It was not at all outlandish to me. I treasured
the thought of being able to defend myself, shuddering at
what it must be like not to be able to do so. To be beaten
or browbeaten without recourse merely because I was
black? Ridiculous and unacceptable. I learned to regard it
as such from Malcolm X. Such is my debt to him. I was a
good student on this matter, as I had no bad habits to
break. I hadn't had to bend to the real world of then. I
saw Robert Penn Warren knew this:

> It may be argued that the personal fate of Malcolm
> X—how much power or what kind of power he
> attains—is not what is important about him. What is
> important may be the mere fact of his existence in
> this moment, his role, his symbolic function.
> I may approach this notion by a story told me by
> Dr. Anna Hedgeman of the National Council of
> Churches. In a seminar she was conducting on race
> and religion there was a serious-minded and idealis-
> tic young white girl from, I think, Alabama. Among
> various guests who spoke at the seminar was Mal-
> colm X . . . The girl asked him if there wasn't any-
> thing she could do—not anything to be acceptable.
> "Not anything," he said. At that she burst into tears.
> Later Dr. Hedgeman said to her: "My dear, don't

you think it strange that you couldn't stand for one minute to be repudiated by that Negro man, when I, like all Negroes, have had to spend my whole life being repudiated by the white race?"

There is something of that little white girl in all of us. Everybody wants to be loved. The member of the White Citizens Council always gets around to telling you how Uncle Billie just loved the kids, would have cut off his right hand for 'em, and how Aunt Sukie or Sallie just loved the whole family and they loved her right back and when she died they all cried and buried her in the family burying ground. But Malcolm X, even now, will have none of this. That stony face breaks into the merciless, glittering leer, and there is not anything, not a thing, you—if you are white—can do, and somewhere deep down in you that little girl is ready to burst into tears. Malcolm X makes you face the absoluteness of the situation.

But Malcolm X, in his symbolic function, does something else, quite paradoxical. Besides the little girl, there is in you too that hard, aggressive, assertive, uncompromising, masculine self that leaps out of its deep inwardness to confront Malcolm X with a repudiation as murderous as his own, saying, "OK, OK, so that's the way you want it, let her rip!" We must confront that wild elation in ourselves: "Let her rip! . . . So, for the white man, Malcolm X can bring the unseen, even the unsuspected, into light. The white man can know what he has to deal with, in himself. So it is for the Negro . . .

And so there were these two imperfect men, King and Malcolm X, touched by a divine and perfect light. Equality, nonviolence and peace, self-sustenance, self-determination and self-defense. Great philosophies got them shot, but they got their message across. They were my leaders.

I have never felt that way about any other black leader,

and there are many other people who I both suspect and know feel the same way. Jesse Jackson was a disciple of King. Louis Farrakhan's mentor was Malcolm X. You can listen to them talk if you don't believe me. But being in the image of a person is not being that person, and now those two are faced with the philosophy of economics, and that is a cause less noble than of their predecessors.

There is a thick layer of people of color in America, thousands and thousands of hard-working people, thinking people, striving people, who were taught long ago by the greatest black leaders of all that leadership is a statement which is not limited to the heart and soul of any one man or woman. King and Malcolm always made a point of that. They were not always going to be around, and it should not matter. Pride and dignity are personal traits. So make your own leadership. Lead your own way. We heard. There are a million black leaders. Maybe more. It's hard to tell because most of us are doing our best to stay out of the newspapers, off television and away from White House state dinners.

We have things to do.

What to See in the South

So, ya wusht ta know whut to see while you visitin the South? Ya come ta the right place. Have some lemonade. Why no sir and no ma'am, lemonades on the house roun heah.

You kin see nearbout whatever you wont ta see down heah in the South. You kin smell rain and honeysuckle, take a walk and see whut you might see. You wont me ta be mo specific? Well, if you in a hurry I cain hep ya. Directions takes time. I cain see why people wont ta come back heah ta visit noways. Ain nuthin here fo em cept some good weather en nothin ta do. They done already tol me that when they lef heah. I tol em they be comin back fuh some fresh air sooner ah later. They don member that part a leavin. But then agin, I kno why they left. Ahm glad they did. I lef too, in mahday. Come back afta I got ol. Jes wonted to res is all. I jus wisht peoples wouldn seem so happy bout leavin when ney come back ta visit. Seem like it embarrass black folk.

One a the reasons I marrid mahthirdwife in the firs place was so she couldn say she didn have relative in the South no more. She from Pencilvania. God's country, let her tell it.

I learnt mos otha black folks feel the same bout the

South. I been roun too, and I got the feelin black folks feel they got one strike on em cause they black, bein from the South jes make strike two. Well, spite the inherent disadvantages . . . hey, boy, don laugh at me. You laughin at yo own self. Don sume nuthin bout me jus cause I talk the easy way some time. Cause I read a book fo yo daddy did. Us folk from the South sometimes do turn out, altho we don't figure South had nuthin ta do wid it till we grow up inside.

The part of the South where I grew up was one of the wust parts ta be in, but I had to hear bout mos of it ta find it out, so it made me strong more then skired me. I grew up dead on top of Miss Sippi, hard by Arkansaw. They got some white folks and hard times in them localities make South Africa look like the fairgroun. If I hadn been in town, ain no tellin. But I was in town. So much fo if. I wuz only in a fix if I didn know where I was goin, and I usually did kno that if nothin else. Directions takes time.

Sometime I woud go downtown to the Malco thee-ater, where my party and me watched matinees from the balcony. I figured the balcony was the bes place, but I was a chile who didn kno betta. Anyway, the Malco was jus en option. The W. C. Handy thee-ater wuz through one fig tree, crost one fence and one screet away from my backyard. I sat anywhere I wonted in the W. C. Handy and didn kno the difference either. It ain there no more The South is a good place ta grow up. But after you grown, a change of locale used ta be avisible if you wont ta put in practice what you learnt as a chile. So peoples been known ta do jus what y'all did. Move on.

Why North, tho? I think trappins has a lot ta do with it. Trappins has messed up lots o folk in the cities in the North. Ya hear a lotta noise, ya see a lotta flash, ya figurs somethin mus be goin on, ya go out ta investigate, pretty soon ya part n parcel of whatever it is. But you don learn a lot cept how to survive the hard way out in nem screets.

Nem screets takes they toll on you. In the South, there wasn that much noise on the screet, so you began to learn ta do something out o sheer boredom. Sang, cobble a shoe, play the piano, baseball, work on a car, thank, whatever. What I learn? Never mine n I might get to it.

The people who looked after you was always on you bout eatin right and bein home at a certain time and goin out to git fresh air and mowin lawns and havin home trainin. You got ta run in the grass jes bout whenever you felt like it, you could hear yourself thank at night and the teachers at school thought well of you and kinda fond, steada havin nightmares about you. Thus feelin thisaway, they done their dead level best ta teach you somethin, even if you wasn of a mind ta learn. They also knowed your folk before you was even born. That cinched the deal on your education. This didn jus only happen ta me. I knows that much. I got lotsa comp'ny. It's jus that we lef the South and stories like the one I jes tol you don go over so well in nem other places, cause didn they lynch black people in the South? Why, yeah, truf, mattah of fac, they did. Thas how black people in the South learnt what some white peoples was capable of. Knowledge come eaurly. In the great northern cities people been lynched, too. They jus didn use no rope.

S'like what happen to that pretty little Brawley child. Got kidnapped fa fo days, raped by five or six mens, had her hair cut off, had somebodys bowel movements rubbed in her hair. This didn happen in '55 in Wes Tennessee. This happen at aroun Thanksgivin time in 1987, and it happen up in New Yawk State, eighty mile fuhtha up from New Yawk City, somewheres outside Poughkeepsie, New Yawk, place call Wappingers Falls or somethin like that. God's country. Girl said one of the mens was a police. Said he had a badge. Made her go wid im. Girl was gone fo five days. Had *Nigger Nigger* and *KKK* wrote on her body in ink or charcoal when they foun her. But you know ink or charcoal wash off. Girl coulda been dead.

Limp till today. Cheerleader I heard, pretty as could be. Some white people in Poughkeepsie try ta act like it didn happen. Jus don b'lieve it. Said so. Town librarian was a white woman name Frances Drace. She say "It's never happened before in this town and some people refuse to believe it." Wellz*somethin* happen to the girl. I don care who dun it. Somethin happened to the girl. Two days after she foun, white man named Harry Crist, spose ta be a part-time police in them parts, committed sideways. Soun like a clue to me.

But, naw, AHM from the South and don kno nothin. Cain even keep a secret. You can look at a mans face and know how he feels in the South. Ain that considered a disadvantage where you livin now, where is that, up in Ohiya? But, see, white man there, ain no surprise ta him when you can do a job good as him. He knowed that when you got there. You wasn the fust ta go, you know. Tol you I been roun. So he smile at you while he hold you down and you don know the diffunce. But that white man in the South, you worry him, you see it on his face. Down here thas considered an advantage. And when he see you can do the job good as him, why that go agains what his people taught him, so he ain so skired of it. He always knowed they was wrong. The ones that don't know and go long with they parents, they go on off and be the Ku Kluk Klan. You can spot em from a mile away, let everybody in town know and cut off trouble fo it start.

If it ain't five-to-one in they favor, or a girl, them Klan boys don even show up. They ain xactly brave yknow.

Fah as black people goes, I don't know why the South drains the chacter and intelligence right outta us the way it do down here. Must have somethin ta do with the river, the Miss Sippi, ta which all others flow. The dirt roun the river must not be good, cause strange storytellin like Richard Wright and Ernest Gaines n Alec Haley. All from nearbouts the river. Made me wisht it hadda got me too.

Them racists over in Alabama drove that pretty Angela

Davis girl right through lotta colleges. All she did was keep her head. Alabama, L.A., lower Alabama, a Bamma from Bama. That sho was Angela, wasn it? In baseball the state of Alabama woud beat everybody with just three ballplayers, Aaron, Mays and McCovey. Notice how they was just roun fo a few years fo they faded on way. Iss the chacter. Black people from the South jus don't have the normal kine.

And health, why, black people from the South are jus pitiful healthy-wise. Look at them legs on that Tina Turner gal. She call herself Tina now, fo the world, cause don't nobody want ta hear bout no country girl name no Anna Mae Bullock from no Nut Bush, Tennessee. But thats ol Anna Mae all right. Know them legs anywhere. Woman older than some of these trees and still got legs a white man ull kill fo. Musta been her diet or somethin. Anna Mae didn even know how to grow ol on time. People from the South is known for that.

We slow down here. We is that. Ol' Bob Hayes from down Flah'ida way took a whole 9.1 seconds to run one hundred yards. He was coarched in college by another slow Southern man, ol' Jake Gaither, who only won two hundred-odd games and loss only fo five whilst he wus at Flah'ida A&M. Ol' Bob won Olympic gold medals, made a pro football team call the Dallas Cowboys worth lookin at, set all kine of records, did some time in the penitentiary and come out lookin like he was still only bout thirty years old, not a wrinkle or a pimple scar on his face. Bob Hayes seem like he been round forever, but hes still a young man. That Wilma Rudolph girl too. Girl had the polio and nineteen or twenty brothers and sisters. Girl run like a deer in the en. Still pretty till dis day.

And sanging? Well, theres a boy or girl or man or woman every other block round here that can sang as sweet as my nature. That Leontyne Price from Miss Sippi even sang a little opera, but I knowdt fo five girls grew up with Leontyne in Miss Sippi could sang just like that.

Jame Earl Jones from there. That Gil Scott-Heron boy,
that boy who like to sing about New Yawk City n stuff?
That boy from right over there in Jackson, Tennessee.
Many's the day I sent that boy home from the recration
center and kept im from shootin dice and messing with
them gals. I usta know all his folk, caust I stayed over
there in Jackson for a while, way back when. That Maya
Angelou, she from Arkansaw. 'Ol Otis Redding from
Georgia. Him and Joe Louis and Revund King. And ol'
Nat Love, that old black cowboy they used to call Dead-
wood Dick? That was way fo yo time. That boy from
right over there in Wes Tennessee. Ma home. Louis
Armstrong from down New Orleans way. That Muham-
mad Ali, he from up in L'ullville. And the Cahalinas?
Cahalinas full of black folk who know how to do
somethin. Thurgood Marshall come from there. Andy
Young and Maynard Jackson, too. Why, wouldn be no
Atlanta if it wudn for Cahalina. Ol Billie Holiday from
Ballemo. Ol Fred'rick Douglass from over that way too.
There was even one or two folk turned out right outta
Virginia. I don't kno everythin bout it, but I could keep
on goin all day. I see you in a hurry. I know. Be spicific.

If you askin me what ta see down here in the South, I
say take a look at the chilren you meets. Take a good
lawng look at em. Cause they growin up ta be somebody
someday. That ain me talkin either. Thas jus the fac of
life.

Member that when you back in Ioway, or wherever
that is you spose ta be livin now. Lawd love ya.

I'm Not ...

I am not a politician, therefore I don't know where to go to have political buttons made up. If I did, I surely would go there now. I would be out the door this minute, on my way to ordering up about fifty million buttons for black people. The buttons would say in simple, uncertain terms.

I'M NOT. . . .

Next to I'M NOT would be a space for the black button wearer to write in the necessary name of the moment. These buttons would cut down on confusion, because of the sad tendency of white people to think that every black person they meet is just like the last black person they saw.

For example, if you are trying to negotiate a labor contract, or just trying to get a raise from a white boss or a loan from a white bank, you need a button that says:

I'M NOT GENE UPSHAW

If you are an actor, you need a button that says:

I'M NOT EDDIE MURPHY . . . BUT I MIGHT KNOW HIM

If you are stopped by a policeman for some traffic violation, whether real or imagined, you need a button:

I'M NOT CARRYING NARCOTICS

If you want to be President, you need:

I'M NOT JESSE

If you're thinking of converting to Judaism, you need:

I'M NOT SAMMY DAVIS, JR.

If you want to be an educator, you need:

I'M NOT JOE CLARK

If you want to be a baseball hitter, you need:

I'M NOT JOE CLARK

If you want to be a dancer, you need:

I'M NOT BEN VEREEN OR MICHAEL JACKSON

If you just want to be left alone, you need:

I'M NOT READY FOR NO DAMN PAROLE BOARD

If you want to attract more attention, you need:

I'M NOT REALLY BLACK—THIS IS JUST A PHASE

If you want a taxi, you need:

I'M NOT HEADING UPTOWN

If you are African, you may need these:

I'M NOT KUNTA KINTE or I'M NOT IDI AMIN DADA

There would also be a universal button:

I'M NOT WHO YOU THINK I AM

If you want to be a writer, you'd probably want this:

I'M NOT RALPH WILEY, AND THANK GOD

If you want to work in the cabinet of the next administration, you will need a button that says:

I'M NOT FOR SALE

Unless of course you are for sale, in which case you're
on your own.

John Thompson

I was anxious to meet John Thompson. I hadn't felt such unilateral confusion, open dislike, heated rancor, unswerving loyalty and good faith toward a black man in American athletics since the days of Muhammad Ali. America told a lot about itself through John Thompson, so I figured this must be a man worth knowing. At the same time, I didn't feel I would get to know the essence of Thompson. I would know no more than what he ever lets the world know. He feels it is enough for us to know he can coach the game, coach all the false air and pride out of it, and reduce it to its essentials.

It was enough we knew he would win seven times out of ten. John Thompson had proven it while coaching the basketball team at Georgetown University. He and his teams had given college basketball history three of its greatest championship games. His teams lost two of those three games, by a total of three points. Even this didn't mellow the general public's attitude toward Thompson. He also won one of the games. This was too great or small a percentage. Thompson seemed to touch people inside, like Muhammad Ali, and I hoped he could reveal to me how he accomplished this, since it seemed to be satisfying and profitable work.

Thompson is a six-foot-ten-inch man of imposing physical proportions, but surprisingly lithe, with a gracefulness undeniable in his movements, especially when he strode on and off the court before a Georgetown game. A big man, as always, but somehow smaller than he is always pictured until you glance at that massive head and the sadness naturally constructed around his eyes. If his expression is blank, he looks precisely as though something is troubling him.

Thompson had been educated in the cream of white institutions—John Carroll High School in Washington, Providence College, the Boston Celtics, coach at St. Anthony's, another Catholic high school, and finally as coach for the team at the Jesuit university. When he was in elementary school, the story went, Thompson had been tested and found not to have high intelligence. This was only the beginning of the insults, which would always occur no matter how well-meaning people were. There was no way for a man the size and complexion of Thompson to hide from this, so he decided not to try.

Whatever Thompson became as he reached forty-six, he had white institutions to thank for it, at least in part. He'd known rejection, so when his time came he carried no guilt for doing his own rejecting. He rejected any notion he had to explain his actions to the national media or anybody else. He was civilized. He did his job supremely. This was his reply, his revenge of living well.

He liked to be seen as a serious, taciturn sort, gruff even, as I found on our first meeting, which came in 1984. Then I was there to see Patrick Ewing, the seven-foot center who was thought to be the personification of Thompson on the court. The second time I met Thompson, two years later, he was still playing gruff. Again, I was not there to see him *per se*, but Reggie Williams, another Georgetown All-American player. It was still Thompson I wished to know.

But John tests you first. He tells you he doesn't have the

time or inclination for you. Just as he was once told, at
face value, by voice, thought, action and innuendo. And
he had to overcome that, survive that, make people see
him through that lens. So he merely asks the same of you.
If you become insulted by his lack of care, and then leave
in a huff, and resent him, well, then he has done what he
wished to do. He has made you feel as he felt. If you stay
with it, eventually he gives you what you need. I stayed
with it.

The third time I met Thompson, we spoke at length,
and pleasantly. He spoke earnestly, even though we never
did shake hands at those meetings. How one could test his
intelligence and find it lacking was beyond me. The man
was a fountain of ideas, theories, thoughts, anecdotes. I
asked him what he made of people saying he was intimidating.

"I try not to spend too much time evaluating or defending John Thompson. It's more important to me to do that
which I feel is correct. I leave the rest to other people. It's
been my experience that people, regardless of being white
or black, have come to me and told me they didn't like
something I said, or commended me on something I said.
I don't think John Thompson can ever say the thing or do
the thing that will win all the people over. Christ came
down here and couldn't do that. I don't expect John
Thompson to do that. The most important thing for me is
to be as honest as I can and to reveal the truth as I perceive it. I can't worry if a member of the media comes in
and has a negative experience with me and then tries to
define me.

"I've been with me for forty-six years and can't define
me. It's impossible for someone to come in and have one
experience with me and declare, 'This is who John
Thompson is.' I'd like to think I'm more complicated than
one meeting."

When I asked Thompson about some white people who
had questions about how many white players he would

have on the U.S. Olympic team in 1988, he smiled and said:

"I personally feel that when you ask a black person that question, it is intended to make the victim the criminal. That's a very tactless question. What it implies is that I am committing a criminal act against someone else and it is very misleading. To my knowledge, black people never held anyone in slavery in this country. The question is used to turn that part of your life around in which you were the victim, making you appear to be the person who committed the crime. The crime was committed against black folks. So I don't feel the need to explain to anybody what the racial makeup of my team will be. I feel I'm fair enough as an individual to know those people, regardless of who is white or black, best capable of bringing home the Olympic gold medal to the United States. Although it would be a lot easier if I had Patrick Ewing and Michael Jordan. I do feel those questions are ploys to turn your role in society around.

"That's what I feel. I will not have a quota. No one picks my team or gives me quotas. Nobody has ever gone to my son and asked him how he feels to be the only black player on the Princeton basketball team. I refuse to be manipulated."

Thompson's team at Georgetown was black by majority. If a white player had the nerve to come out for the team and stay out, Thompson might just keep him. Not if he was weak-minded, though. I had heard stories where recruiters from other colleges would make sure that any white player talented enough to really play for Georgetown would never consider it. The recruiters accomplished this by saying, "Oh, you don't want to go *there.*" Thompson was not angered by this. He was a tactician. He admired tactics. He would put a team on the floor. He'd win with what he had.

What Thompson had were kids of all different classes. Unfortunately, class has become synonymous with money.

This has been an unworthy fate for class. To me, class has to do with choice, taste, carriage, grooming, manner and the like. But household income, holdings and inheritances determine class in America. By my own measure, if a young man was not at least middle class when he came to Georgetown to play for John Thompson—and a few of them who did already were—then he surely would be by the time Thompson got through with him. Anytime Georgetown's teams traveled, they were impeccably dressed, carried themselves ramrod-straight and kept noise down. They lived with the school's general population in the dormitories. They were not a band of physically gifted ragamuffins there to perform a minstrel show for free. They were there to do business.

What Thompson's teams demonstrated, above all, was a certain discipline. No need to wonder about this discipline's origin. I felt this made some uneasy. Power can be so vain it believes there can be no order unless power brings order. Without power, there can only be chaos. Thompson verified this as myth, even as his teams were labeled desperately chaotic by powers that be. Order brings power. If a young man spent four years at Georgetown, he left with class.

Inevitably, all of this only helped the public marketing of John Thompson and college basketball. He liked to say, "I don't care what people think. As long as they come inside." Thompson was easy for white people to embrace as a villain, I felt. It took no thought for them to dislike him. He was as black as Darth Vader, or Black Monday, or devil's food cake, or any other of those negative metaphors so popular in our time. And his teams were always, always excellent. Even in his down years he'd somehow win twenty, and a victory over Georgetown was celebrated with a special verve. Like Ali and Darth Vader before him, Thompson sold tickets.

He also made white people see themselves more clearly in relation to their own assumptions of liberalism. When the Georgetown team was involved in the occasional on-court fight or brawl, Georgetown basketball was called violent, and Georgetown basketball was John Thompson. After the 1988 season, a rule against brawls came into college basketball. The Georgetown rule. People had even made claims that the Georgetown teams were the only ones ever involved in fights. This was how ridiculous it became. Meanwhile, people would conveniently forget fights like the one between Syracuse and Providence in the Final Four in 1987, or by Yale and Dartmouth any year.

These incidents were forgotten, even later remembered fondly, as they should have been, for in fact sometimes in the heat of competition these things will happen. Boys will be boys. One presumed writer in a New York newspaper, whose dislike of Thompson apparently knew only distant bounds, wrote that the fact Thompson's players usually graduated and stayed out of drug rehab and went on to do positive things was not the point. The writer said the point was that of the last ten fights on a basketball court he had seen, Georgetown had been involved in all of them.

Apparently the writer closed his eyes any time other teams scuffled on the court. To say this scuffling was the point of anything was doubly racist. In the first place, the writer must have believed the only thing black people were cut out to do was play basketball, if getting into a scuffle on the court was more important than becoming a judge. And it was flagrantly racist to deny that other teams scuffle.

In fact, most of the scuffles involving Georgetown came because, like Thompson himself, his Hoyas rarely backed down. In most cases, the Hoyas played the game better than the teams they faced. The Hoyas were coached better. When being bested, a player does whatever is necessary to remain competitive. Such is the nature of competition in some. Some will elbow, shove, scratch, reach, talk about your mother and anything else, because playing pure basketball against a John Thompson team was to invite defeat. Thompson's teams played for forty minutes, ninety-four feet, end line to end line, and had been taught the details of man-to-man defense by one of the great masters. So when confronted by the tactics of survival against the unrelenting pressure, the Hoyas didn't back off.

What is rarely underscored about Thompson is that he takes his defeats so well. He was congratulatory toward the Villanova coach, Rollie Massimino, much as he had been toward Dean Smith, whose North Carolina team, led by Michael Jordan, beat Georgetown in the championship game in 1982, probably the greatest championship game ever played. When a Georgetown player, Fred Brown, threw the ball to a North Carolina player, James Worthy, by mistake in the final seconds, Thompson embraced Brown on the court.

A year after the 1985 Georgetown-Villanova championship game, it came out that Gary McLain, the Villanova point guard, was taking cocaine all through the week of the championship game. Thompson was such a strong father figure that his players rarely if ever succumbed to such behavior while in college. If they had, he would have known it and it would not have been tolerated. Another player, Len Bias, expired on the campus of the University of Maryland while using cocaine. This part of Thompson's teaching process and prowess was rarely examined, because it went against the villainous image, which was so easy and profitable.

Meanwhile, black people not directly involved seemed just as unanimous in their support and outright love for Thompson as white people were in their dislike. All of this made for great American theater and a tremendous profit, not only for television and the NCAA, but also for Georgetown and John Thompson. "I'd like to be remembered as a teacher," Thompson said. "And I'd like to be rich. I stress to my young men that we are in a capitalistic system where the object is gain for work done." To that end, Georgetown hung the professional NBA jerseys of its basketball graduates in McDonough Arena, the home of the Hoyas, on the Washington, D.C., campus of the great Jesuit university where a black man was a loud, difficult and ultimately beneficent king.

"Well, I haven't spent a lot of time thinking about how people perceive me. I am six-foot-ten-inches, I'm black, I'm loud. If you see a big tree in the forest that has large roots, it makes an impression on you. I have large hands, large mouth, make big sounds. Even if I'm not angry, I am loud, and saying what you feel, some people are going to perceive that as intimidating. I cannot control what a person perceives. I know what my intentions are. I feel it is important to say the things I feel to be correct. I don't intentionally try to hurt anybody's feelings or to intimidate anybody, unless I feel they are trying to offend me purposely. It is important to me to express what I perceive as the truth. Sometimes I'm incorrect. I don't want to go through this experience called education, just to be perceived as a good person. I have to say the truth. The public is more important than the press.

"I don't think of it as making a stand for myself. I just do what comes naturally to me. When I was attending John Carroll High, a person sat up and taught history, philosophy, mathematics. There was no white math or black math. He teaches also justice. What's right and wrong. If you sit in that classroom, and learn these things, why when you see an injustice, you don't think about whether it's white or black. I'm a product of the society that educated me. I was not educated to distinguish that this set of rules go for white people and these for blacks. I don't care where you've been educated. If you came through the American system, you've had experiences which have been degrading if you are an American black man. And I think you don't hold anybody responsible, but I think you are bound to make society aware these things exist when you see they exist."

There was little doubt, in my mind at least, that John Thompson, Dean Smith of North Carolina and Bobby Knight of Indiana were the best college coaches of their time and fairly responsible, for better or worse, for the explosion of college basketball as a televised entertainment entity. Thompson and Knight were considered ogres by some, but Knight had much, much more rope.

If Thompson had thrown a chair across a court, or taken his team off the court and quit cold in a game against the Russians, or snatched players by their jerseys during games, or, no matter how innocently, talked about relaxing while enjoying rape—my God, you can imagine the reaction. John Thompson would have been run out of town. That was my assumption. But if Thompson *had* done things of that nature, they would have been calculated. He would have survived. Thompson seemed to do nothing without a reason. He was very controlled, and seemed to live a very structured life. There was very little wasted motion of any kind in his daily schedule, and he didn't spend time bowing to social conventions, other than the manners his parents had bestowed on him. His bark was much more severe than his bite.

Thompson was going to win seven times out of ten as surely as the sun was going to rise the next day. So the continuum of the public reaction to him was assured, as was the continuation of Georgetown basketball and the final realization of his desire to become rich. The irony is this: My given was that white people removed from Thompson nearly unanimously despised him, either secretly or out loud, and black people removed from Thompson, either secretly or out loud, always wished him the best, always figured he was right and wanted his team to be the best.

But Thompson felt that white people close to George-town were his most solid allies. "It is my own people, black people, who try to do us harm from close," he said. I must admit that after considering it, this illumination did not exactly stun me.

I told him, or rather I suggested to him, that surely he was aware that this was not uncommon. Thompson allowed that. This manifestation of self-hatred was not directed at him, or his terrible burden to bear alone, warping only his judgment, but was a binding generality. He also made it plain that he would be sabotaged for no one. Not even for old times' sake. Not even if some things changed.

John Thompson was able to extract the essence of most American people, make us all so obvious and translucent to each other, if only we would pay attention to ourselves and our visceral reactions to this one man. Thompson had convinced himself few of us mattered to him because he didn't like what he saw when he pulled out the essence of his fellow men. What he did find seemed to motivate him.

This is why Thompson assumed nothing about people, went so far, was so vilified, so honored, so respected and even, in a strange way, was needed by Americans, much as people later found they loved and respected Muhammad Ali. Thompson was just a coach, just a teacher, in fact, one of the few teachers paid an appropriate scale in this society of wasted motions and vain ideas of class. I knew that somewhere out there an impatient boy or girl was watching, listening to the drum, waiting for a chance to do what Thompson does, only better. In the end, this is what made Thompson just as valuable an icon in his time as Ali had been in his.

Black people knew they could fight and scuffle, and be proud of their independence. What Thompson demonstrated was how well black people can teach. Maybe he'd make teaching popular. Maybe that was too much to ask of us. Unfortunately, I've never been to a basketball game where a seminar broke out unless Georgetown was involved.

About Travel

How Black People Do on IQ Tests

Once I took an adventure to Martinique. It was just in my mind to go there, like a beckoning. Martinique sounded beautiful and mysterious, so I made plans to go. I suppose I wanted to be mystified. I received my wish. While I was in Martinique, I found out I was an idiot. This is doubly mortifying when you have been walking around with a high opinion of yourself. I failed the IQ test in Martinique. Now another high horse and my fascination with mystery are gone.

Martinique, for those of you who do not know, is one of the blue-green jewels of the Caribbean, an island more mountainous than all the other islands of the Caribbean, save Jamaica itself. Martinique is also considered a French possession. When I found out Martinique was a French possession, I was still in California. The information seemed incidental. Hah.

Upon disembarking in Martinique, I immediately took my place as an idiot, for I do not speak French at all. I knew this would be a problem when a taxi driver said something to me. I looked at him in confusion. The man was speaking gibberish. But it sounded good, melodious, and he waited for a reply. I had none to give him, except a smile and a look of helplessness. He cringed, made a face and turned away.

I knew how to say only one thing in French, and this was that I didn't speak French. I did not even say this well. After being led through the day by my attractive translator and traveling companion (remember, I was not an idiot until I reached Martinique), I was ready for dinner. If you had asked me what *poisson* was before I went to Martinique, I would have told you it is what will kill you if you eat it. Unfortunately, the people of Martinique often have *poisson* for dinner. My attractive translator lowered her lashes and said *poisson* meant fish, but I was becoming suspicious of her. She spoke French reasonably well and many of the local men had engaged her in conversations which didn't seem to include me. But since my translator was my only companion, I had to trust her. I didn't like being at the mercy of anyone but me. I happen to know how people usually treat idiots.

During my three eternal days as the village idiot of Fort-de-France, I cursed myself for having chosen Spanish as my foreign language of study in high school and college. The instructors had made all the difference there. Mrs. Barbara Jo Savage was my high school Spanish teacher, and she was lively and good at her job and there were times I had a crush on her. I don't even remember the high school French teacher. That's how close I came to taking French. Mrs. Savage didn't do badly. I have been to Spanish-speaking countries and only been stupid. In French, I was a moron. This was very sad, but unimpeachably true.

Soon I left Martinique, thinking about the intelligence quotient tests people are always making a fuss about. What they mean or prove. Martinique determined for me that IQ tests are fairly useless. If you don't speak or read the language, you don't have a prayer of being intelligent. I thought about the people who said that IQ tests in

America were "culturally biased" against black people. I thought about the first night in Martinique, when several small lizards were running around the inn where I was staying.

When asked *"What do you do when several small lizards run around the room while you're trying to sleep?"* a person from Martinique might answer (a) Ignore them. I answered (d) Leave the vicinity. I got the answer wrong. This was a fine inn, near the beach, rustic and secure, with an excellent chef. My translator was happy. But I was ignorant to the ways and the lay of the land and the language. I wanted to go to a hotel with no lizards, so I did. It had no lizards. Other than that, it was a terribly depressing place to stay. (d) Leave the vicinity, had been the wrong answer.

A person can be tested for knowledge and have the results measured properly, but not for intelligence. Back in America, I always did well on intelligence tests. This made me think I was smart. Now I know I was merely lucky to have taken the test where I had read a few books and been familiar with several forms of the language and culture. If I had been given the same tests in French, in Martinique, I would have found out where I really stood.

What Black People Should Do When Going Through New York City

First of all, you have to know how to carry yourself in New York City. You have to know how to hurry. If you're not in a hurry, you won't go very far in New York. At the same time, you must carefully watch your step. If you don't watch your step, you won't be able to look up, and if you don't look up every now and then, something may fall on you and kill you.

It happens several times a year. A two-by-four falling on you and killing you can only happen in New York. The same two-by-four can fall and hit you on the head in Cleveland and just give you a headache. In New York, everything falls so far.

Once you are indoors in New York, you're fine. As long as you know what you're talking about. Never hesitate. If you hesitate in New York City, not only are you lost, your belongings are going to be gone for sure. And you'll never get anything on sale to replace them if you don't hurry.

If you at least have a firm question, you'll just be hollered at and told to move along. If you don't know what you're talking about, act like you speak a foreign

language. Like Philadelphian. That way people don't
know if you know anything or not. They give you the
benefit of the doubt.

It's always best to know what you're talking about in
New York. If you can't manage this, act as if you know.
That way you can get paid. That's the way New York
works. You've got answers? You get paid. You can get paid
and be treated like a king if you can hit a baseball or
shoot world-class hoop or tap dance, and you don't have
to know anything at all.

You should don soft shoes in New York. You can wear
out a pair of feet right up to the ankle just walking from
here to right over there in New York. That's why New
Yorkers have an undeserved reputation for bad attitudes.
They're usually portrayed in the afternoon or evening,
and by then, after pounding that concrete of concretes,
here comes "Live at Five" for an on-the-street interview.

New Yorkers don't have bad attitudes. Their feet hurt.
So they talk like it. The most popular doctors in New York
are podiatrists. They left the shrinks in their dust. Don't
ask for trouble and doctor bills. Never walk anywhere in
New York when you can ride.

If you must walk, talk to yourself. This will discourage
the muggers, panhandlers, vigilantes, prostitutes and con
artists, and may get you hired by an advertising agency.

If you ride the subways, never sit near any young black
men, for they are about to be shot on sight, and you along
with them if you're not watching your step as you should
be. If you are a young black man, you're going to be
more on your own than you've ever been, especially on
the subway.

If I tried to list all of a black person's New York here,
I'd never finish. There always something new. In Manhattan, you can do just about anything, anytime, with anybody, anywhere, as long as you make enough noise.

If you can think of it, it's in New York. The ballet and
ensemble companies, midtown, downtown, the Village

jazz clubs, the West Side and Harlem if you know where you're going, especially the Schomburg Center. Take a good look at Harlem. A lot of people didn't look up and hesitated, but the heroin flights were always right on schedule.

So Harlem isn't what it used to be. Somebody made off with its belongings. But it's still better than the East Side. I would not recommend the East Side. You tend to be blamed over there. If it's raining, it's going to be your fault. If you're going to the other boroughs of New York around Manhattan, it must be to Brooklyn or the Bronx to hang out with some of the folks. Other than that, you must have a good reason. Just don't let the reason be a sudden taste for pizza in Howard Beach, Queens, unless you're a lawyer or an anthropologist. And beware the Haitian cab driver. He will only take you where you do not want to go. And you can't even yell at him like a good New Yorker, because in your heart you know it's not his fault. It's the environment.

One other thing: Once you come to Harlem, part of you will never leave. There's no charge for this curiously wonderful bargain. It seems to come along with the tolls.

White People's Most Admirable Trait

Judging from some of what I've read, the most admirable trait of some white people is their ability to treat black people fairly, as peers even, of having no truck with racial prejudice of any kind. This conduct apparently elevates them. Many politicians, movie directors, football coaches and other public persons have been written up in this light. It sounds so soothing and reassuring. Whenever I've read the best-done feature stories by some of my colleagues in the media, describing the lives of these great humanitarians, I can count on some proof of how even-handed and fair they were. This is supposed to be a sort of proof of one of the three most enviable human traits, along with talent and the ability to lie convincingly. That trait is compassion.

I would like to meet some of these fair and compassionate white people. I suppose I've usually been in the wrong places at the wrong times. Too often I find that the hardest thing for a white person to do is show respect to a black person who isn't famous, and act normal while other white people are standing around looking. They have a couple of words for white people like that, and

they aren't "Nice going." Actually, I have met quite a
number of white people with the most admirable trait.
The odd thing is most of those I have met happened to be
in California at the time. I don't know why this is so, but
I suspect it has something to do with a combination of the
weather and the fact that the West has always represented
a new start, a new world, a place where one didn't have
to act as one had been taught to act.

This tendency isn't hard and fast. In early 1987, it came
to light that a photograph of twenty-odd San Francisco
firemen who had been honored for heroism had been
altered. One face and body was obliterated from the picture. Needless to say, the obliterated fire fighter was the
only black person in the picture. Or, he had been before
the photo doctor—a transplanted Easterner, no doubt—
had corrected history in his own fashion. In all, it made
me wonder if people like that worked for King James's
Bible revisionists.

It's not that I didn't try to find some white people in the
East with this trait. I most surely did. And I came up
with a couple of really good ones. They are some of my
best friends. But, if you are a perfectionist, as I am, you
always think about the one who got away.

I thought I had one for sure. He was one of my colleagues, one who often wrote stories describing how sensitive his subjects were to people different from themselves.
But, as I sensed, this wasn't compassion he was talking
about. This was like saying the subject had an enviable
trait that might actually be a cross to bear, a burden,
which would make the subject more sympathetic, more
worthy of compassion.

The largest group of people who think something of
themselves find you not difficult to bear at all and will
pity you plenty—until you're doing the same job just as
well. Then competition, being competition, will seek out
flaws in character.

One night, as I advanced on a white Famous Ego-

Tripper for my own purposes of gathering quotes, my colleague, who thought he had the Greatest Trait but actually didn't any more than the next man, gave me a look that wasn't saying "Nice going." It was at a dinner honoring both of them, my author colleague and his subject, plus a few lesser lights of society. I happened to be in Boston, and I needed a quote from this Famous Ego-Tripper my colleague had written about. Apparently my colleague thought for some reason I shouldn't be doing this, though I had chosen an informal moment, when the Famous Ego-Tripper was between speeches, drinks and other social obligations, to ask my questions.

I have met white people who did have the great trait, however, and in the genuine sense. I will not do them the dishonor of bragging on them about it. They know who they are. It is pleasant, broadening and ultimately profitable to be comfortable in other people's company. I remember being on the road with my white newspaper colleagues, and, all in all, everything was on the up-and-up, even though we were competing just as surely as people ever did. But we were from California. It could be worked out. I remember them well, even though things didn't always go well. I think it was because I knew they respected me and they knew I respected them. This is not something you can be told. Respect is acted out.

So whenever I read a feature story in a magazine or newspaper or book and it gets to the part where So-and-So wouldn't let this black person be discriminated against by other people, or how old So-and-So always understood minorities, I disregard it. Old So-and-So could only act for himself on those matters, and only the people who knew him and crossed his path when he was living his life knew whether or not it was true. Words didn't mean a thing. Words serve no true justice.

As for me, I came to the conclusion that white people's most admirable trait was a good attitude about California, even if they hadn't been there. It is an imprecise test, to be sure, but it beats trial and error. I call it the California Test. If the person in question is open to California, or noncommittal, or at least ambivalent about it, then that is enough for me. Just don't stand in the way of progress. But if he says, "God," "Ugh," "How could anyone live there?" "I hated it" or "You actually *liked* that place?" then I watch him very closely when he is in a position to affect how I go about my business. Otherwise, I can't afford to care. People who are wary about the new, about what they don't yet understand or fully comprehend—I can't waste time on them. Let them write stories about each other and exhibit one of the most enviable of human traits. The ability to lie convincingly.

Aliens

A black man may or may not have not been the original sighter of UFOs, but a black man was the first I heard to describe them by race in public. The brother was dressed in a flowing white robe and a bright blue fez and said he was from Detroit. I had no reason to doubt him. He was leaning on a stop sign for dear life not far from downtown Los Angeles, screaming his lungs out. "They ain't *from* here! They ain't *from* here!" he said.

So I had to ask the brother, "Who ain't?" He looked at me as if he didn't know where I had been. "They ain't!" he said before looking furtively over his shoulders at the cars tooling along on Crenshaw Boulevard. "We are. But they ain't."

Then he asked if I wanted to buy some incense.

I asked if it was strong enough to drive Them back.

He laughed and said, "Maybe."

In the black man's case, his belief in "Them" as aliens was a psychological crutch, a balm of sorts. During all those atrocities over all these years, black people were generally stunned into inactivity or, in some cases, into leaning on stop signs and selling incense and prophecy.

At one time the atrocities committed against black people were so unconscionable, and carried out at such a fever pitch and with such relish, that the easiest way to accept them was with a theory which said that those perpetrating these inhuman atrocities were not human. No humans could do that to other humans. Well, isolated cases, maybe. But this madness seemed to go right on across the board. So it must have been Andromedans, Venusians or Alpha Centaurians who were to blame for slavery, apartheid, genocide and politics on Earth. More than one otherwise intelligent black person has said this to me, even though most of them were half joking.

I also sensed that white people embraced the notion that black people were not human. Another psychological crutch. Most white people can read, see and hear. But the easiest way to salve one's conscience—if, indeed, one had a conscience—was to assume those carcasses being dragged through streets were not human, or less human. It made them easier to ignore and make it harder on the live ones.

Some white people probably felt in their hearts they would never allow all this to happen to other humans—not even to the Jewish people or the Irish or even the Italians. Maybe a war, to keep the circulation going. But hundreds of years of debasement and destruction of art and obliteration carried out against fellow humans was utter stuff and nonsense. But then, suppose those people weren't really from here? In that case, they deserved whatever they got.

If white people did see humanity in black people, then white people would be admitting they had been bad for too long to get into heaven or other nice astral places. So some white people either considered black people not human, alien, or they forsook religion. There was no other way to go and stay sane. If black people were human—and we have recent proof which shows it just might be that they are—and religion has a basis in fact, then there are a lot of unredeemable souls out there, asking for a recount.

John Sayles is a white movie director. He seems to be as human as human can get. On October 15, 1987, he was featured in *The Washington Post*, in the "Style" section. The feature story made me look up and wonder. I experienced my disquiet and unease near the end, when The Author of the article, who I had assumed was from Earth, showed herself. Sayles had been quoted thusly by The Author: "Some of [my eclectic view] is having lived in a lot of different places as a kid, in the country and in the city." Here, The Author broke the quote with this: "Sayles muses, trying to explain." Explain what? The fact that he had lived on Earth? Ooo-OOO-ooo.

Sayles's quote was then continued. "I think that gives you some perspective. If you live in the same place it's possible to think, there's Us and there's Them, and They're not like Us. If you move around, sometimes you move into Their neighborhood." Obviously, Johnny Sayles was not talking about Martians here, eh? One paragraph later: " 'I'm sure at some point I'll make stuff about people who are educated and white and that stuff,' Sayles says, a bit uncomfortably." Now, which had made Sayles uncomfortable—the work he had done, or the unblinking visage of The Author?

At that moment, Sayles was wrapping up *Matewan*, a movie about the trials of coal miners. Before that, he made a film called *The Brother From Another Planet*. It was set in Harlem. The plot had to do with a black alien and his alien brethren, both black and white. Personally, I wanted to see if Sayles would have laughed if I had told him he should make a movie entitled *White Man from Another Planet*, about the tribulations of a white alien trapped in first class over Palm Springs. If he laughed, like the brother by the stop sign, then I could know he was human. He probably is anyway. However, I will watch the skies for the likes of The Author. They're out there, and I'm fresh out of incense.

Chicken in a Car

I don't know what motivates children to say the things they say. I think the truth usually has something to do with it. I remember a rhyme we once sang. *Knife and a fork and a plate of greens, that's how you spell New Orleans.*

I never went to New Orleans as a child, so whatever link that rhyme has with the truth is beyond me. I've been to New Orleans, but as a man, not a child, so my feelings about it are pedestrian. I know you can eat well there without once having a plate of greens. New Orleans is a nice place to visit, as long as it isn't summer. I probably should know more about New Orleans, but that was not the way life went.

The other part of the rhyme: *Chicken in a car, car couldn't go, that's how you spell Chicago.*

I'd always known Chicago. The place was talked up and built up by my people when I was a child. Somewhere else people could have been and probably were talking up and building up New York or Detroit or L.A., or even Kansas City or Vallejo, but Chicago was the place to go if you were from my neck of the woods, assuming you went by the word of adults. Everybody was going to Chicago. If you couldn't make it there, you couldn't make it anywhere. It was funny, the way my people would put that.

I know I was in Chicago a great deal of time during my childhood, but I can only remember the summers and the good. We would arrive on the City of New Orleans train. A train is a glamorous way for a child to arrive anywhere, especially a child too young to know or care about segregated railcars. It seemed to me as if Chicago was all it was cracked up to be. Where were all those cars going? Probably to the tall buildings in the distance. Chicago was it, all right.

Then I was not a child, but a college student, and where did I choose to go for summer vacation? Could there be any question? Chicago. Chicago taught me never to trust census data. The census said there were something like thirty million black people in America at the time. I knew better than that. I had seen thirty million black people on the South Side of Chicago in a single weekend when I was twenty.

The South Side of Chicago was Chicago. The downtown Loop was an amusement park. The rest of the city barely existed, then didn't exist, like an early morning dream. The other Chicago might as well have been in Texas, especially when I was a child, although it is only a little different today. Sometimes I have business in Texas now. But not as a child. Chicago is a city of neighborhoods the way Berlin is, except there is no wall to warn you where east doesn't meet west. The unbridled feeling in Chicago is that if you aren't in "your neighborhood" you are spoiling for a fight.

They call New Orleans "Big Easy." I called Chicago "Big Nasty." Chicago was and is what a sociologist would call racially polarized, as if it came with the climate. If you got caught between Poles, you were in trouble. Chicago was the kind of place where you could get a gun put in your face while you were robbed, then have the police roust you when they got there as if you had robbed yourself. Are you sure you didn't stick a gun in your own face and rob yourself? the Chicago police might ask while cracking their knuckles on your head. Chicago was the kind of place where you could be thrown in jail for general principles.

Black people came running to Chicago to be pent up in high-rise projects that stretched for long Chicago blocks, and eventually suffer the consequences of such living arrangements. I hate the sight of those projects. I have been inside them to see a lovely girl. I have been with Chicago for so long that I love it but I can't stand the sight of it. It lives best in my first memory of youth. Only there is it ever so grand.

My great-aunt Spokie died in Chicago. I was too young to know what death was then. All I remember is using one finger to scoop butter off her dish and watching her smile at me and ask me when I would be four. Soon, I told her. I had a cousin named Valerie. We had our picture taken in a carriage at Riverview amusement park. I had a crush on Valerie. I got over it. I was only eight.

I don't know how long the Magikist sign has been there, only that for me it has always been there, those red lips looming over the Dan Ryan expressway, the Damn Ryan, which cut through like a toothache outside the little house at 48 West Eighty-First Street where my uncle Herman and aunt Webbie lived forever after Spokie died. I remember those Magikist lips. They were like Spokie's. I never called her Spokie. I had called her Aunt *Oui*. Aunt Yes. The Magikist lips flashed the time of day beneath them and reassured me as I went out to catch the el or a bus, to ride out and grapple with Big Nasty.

Uncle Herman was a mortician. When I was fourteen, he tried me out on the job. He took me in the A. R. Leak's black hearse to the bottom of a hospital. A bag was lying there on a white table. He opened the bag, grabbed a pair of ankles and pulled out a small girl. He asked me if I could put her back in the bag. I said I really couldn't. I touched her cold leg. I had never touched a dead girl until I came to Chicago. I never knew girls died. Not like this. Was this what happened to Spokie? Was Chicago this cold?

Uncle Herman had his doubts about me after that. But at least he knew I wanted to work. When I was twenty, my friend Roy and I worked through summer vacation at the National Lead Factory, way out on Halsted. Roy was called in for a job. I went with him. Somebody had quit because his job was too dangerous and so I took it, never pausing to ask what made the job dangerous. I didn't even understand when they gave me a respirator to wear over my nose and mouth, with little white filters to go inside. I was to change the filters often.

I was young and immortal and this was Chicago and there was nothing I couldn't do as long as I did it on the South Side. The lead was smelted without pause, and I stacked the cool ingots of slag into stacks of fifty. Five bars wide, five bars deep, ten levels high. The bars were very heavy, but I was young and strong and considered myself well paid. The forklift ran all day. I went and bought cheap shoes with my pay. Our foreman was a white man. In racially polarized Chicago he told my friend Roy and me to go back to college when the summer ended, that we didn't want to do this for the rest of our lives. I was surprised he said this, even though I knew it was true.

My buddy Roy and I had an adventure away from Chicago that summer, as we decided to take the 1963 Corvair which ferried us the blocks to work every morning and put it on the highway to Memphis. We were twenty years old and invincible and we wore big Panama hats to prove it and put the top down on this rather odd convertible and just cruised happily for about two hundred miles or so, just riding and talking and feeling the summer heat.

Just outside of Effingham, Illinois, the car had what for it was a severe stroke. Roy hitched a ride with a trucker

to get to a service station. Meanwhile, his brother
Charles, a cop in Chicago, blew past the hissing, still Corvair in his brand-new Charger. I thought he had missed
me. Soon he came back around the bend. We nursed the
Corvair as far as just below the Missouri bootheel, and
eventually gave it over to a car junk shop, whose owner
was dumb, but not so dumb he didn't realize he had us
over a barrel.

That Corvair would have gotten us to work the rest of
the summer had we left well enough alone and rode with
Charles to Memphis. But we were young and had to try. I
thought of this later when I took the slow Halsted bus to
the National Lead Factory for the remainder of the summer.

Still I came back to Chicago. I wanted to work for a
black publisher when I left college. I went in for a job,
but the young black man who was hiring had little time
to study my offer of service. I suppose if he had looked me
over, he would have hustled me out more quickly. But he
was smitten by a beautiful movie actress who was waiting
for him in the foyer of his office. So he just told me I was
too young. He was twenty-three. I was twenty-three. He
later married the actress.

I couldn't say I blamed him for any of it. I often
wonder what would have happened if he'd hired me. But
he didn't, and so I went to the West Side to find work at
the age of twenty-three, and just by showing up found a
version, as a teller at a credit union. I didn't mind working there other than the fact I knew I wasn't a teller. But
it was a job that at least paid carfare with something left
over and I felt as though I were at least attempting to be
productive and was basically hoping to only do that.
Somehow I would get to the writing.

I was thinking about the writing one Saturday morning
when I came to the credit union, stopping first at the
corner grocery store across the street to pick up something. I was distracted but always noticing what was

around me, even if I didn't notice until later. The shop-keeper was a woman well into her forties, her face worn and twisted by life. She seemed contemptuous of me, even though I brought her a dollar or two every day for her skimpy comestibles. Looking back, I think she knew what was happening. The credit union was being robbed.

I unlocked the door and went into the lobby of the building's one-story bunker. Immediately I was wrapped in a bear hug. The arms were strong but younger and greener, unyielding yet trembling, and since I had played contact sports I reacted in what some people call a natural manner, acted as I had been trained to act, immediately factoring that this was a young person, a boy sixteen or seventeen, and that I could turn and grab his head and try with all my might to twist it off. I wouldn't be in a bear hug long.

The boy cried out and someone jumped from behind the door which led to the interior of the credit union.

I cannot until this day say anything of what this person looked like because he was holding a revolver in both hands and he put the muzzle of the gun six inches away from the bridge of my nose. I ceased my struggle immediately and the boy let me go. I don't know how long we actually stood there, the boy behind me breathing heavily and noisily, me taking no breath at all. The man with the gun, the most important person in the building at that second, was completely devoid of other characteristics as far as I was concerned. The muzzle of the gun had me transfixed. This was it. There was no feeling in me what-soever other than knowing this was it. I don't recall whether it was death or life or reality or just what it was.

Then the person with the gun said, "On the floor." I, entranced, walked into the interior of the credit union, behind the steel door and the thick windows.

There were two other employees present, a usually pleasant young woman who was the color of toffee and somewhat obese and who tried to run the credit union efficiently, and a young man who was the color of sweetened tea and who also lived in Evanston and was handicapped and needed metal crutches to walk, but never seemed to let this ruin his demeanor. He was a nice man. I could see they both were absolutely petrified.

By then I could tell without looking directly at him that the person with the gun was nothing more than another boy, perhaps not as old as I was at twenty-three. He ordered us to empty the drawers of the perhaps two hundred dollars therein, and then demanded we open the vault and gather up the four or six hundred dollars it contained. Then he announced that he was locking us in the vault.

"No," I said.

He looked at me.

"Put the damn money in the bag."

"Yes, sir."

"Don't yes-sir me. Yes-sir the white man. Git in the damn vault."

"No."

He dropped the bag and some money spilled out. We both kneeled down to stuff the bills back. He laid the gun next to him, a foot away from his hand. Three feet away from mine. I was tempted to try, but I could not see the other boy and by then the greater risk was gone, the gun was back in his hand, the muzzle gaping in my eyes.

"Git on the floor."

We did and they ran out and we got up within a minute and called the police. They came and questioned us and I thought no more of it save the muzzle of the gun, and that would be indelible as it turned out. The robbery was the topic of conversation for the next week, but unless someone at the credit union brought it up, I didn't think about it.

Then the next week the police came back and took the nice woman the color of toffee and the handicapped man the color of tea and then later came and took me. I didn't know where the others had been taken. I was taken to the jail. The police officers were brusque and said I had to take a lie detector test. Since they said so, I presumed I had to take one. I was strapped into the device, with a cord slipped across my chest and metal clasped to my fingertips. I didn't tell them no, as I had told the boy with the gun in my face. Was it that I had nothing to fear from them? I hadn't robbed anything. I was above all innocent.

The questioning began.

"Have you ever done anything wrong?"

"What?"

"Have you ever committed a crime, a robbery?"

My mind raced. I was sure I had committed many, even if they were only small ones. I was sure I had.

"No."

"Have you ever profited from a robbery?"

"No."

"Do you know anyone who has?"

At that moment I began holding my breath, and then releasing it in a rush, clenching and unclenching my fists, breathing in short bursts, anything to attempt to defeat this man. Not the machine. The man. I was asked more questions as the room began to fill with blue tobacco smoke. Soon I was unstrapped and taken to a windowless room where two detectives were waiting for my arrival.

"We know you had something to do with this. The machine said you were lying." The other cop stood over me ominously with a sneer on his face and his hands behind his back. He looked like the muzzle of the gun. The fear left again, just as before. Here it was. I didn't know what—life, death, truth, reality—but it was here. "Did the machine say I was lying about going to college for five years? I just got out. Now, why would I spend five years going to college, get out, and then have something to do with robbing a place?"

The seated cop considered this. The standing cop didn't

hear me. They conferred while I sat. The seated cop said, "We are charging you with suspicion of conspiracy to commit armed robbery." So here it was. "I haven't done anything," I said. The standing cop seemed disappointed, for whatever reason. I was taken to a cell and kept there for five hours. I didn't ask whether or not the charge was legitimate, I didn't ask to make a phone call. I sat in the cell because that was where the police had taken me. After five hours, I was released from the cell. I felt nothing, not relief, not anger. I went back to Uncle Herman and Aunt Webbie's house and told Uncle Herman what had happened. He laughed. He knew I had nothing to do with any robberies, at least recently, but he still laughed. "Now," he said, "you're beginning to see how it is, eh? Now you see."

At the end of the week I went back to the credit union to get my pay. The president of the credit union looked at me and said, "Ralph, why don't you tell us who was in it with you and cleanse your soul." He was a black man the color of a dry lemon and he liked to talk about niggers stealing.

I had no answer for him, and none for Chicago, so I took my pay, thanked no one, and left. And when I went back to visit, which I did like a lemming running to the sea, I tried not to think about my failures, for they said I couldn't make it in Chicago. I wouldn't make it anywhere.

The theory turned out to be false, but only after I grew up and stopped counting years so happily. I had been in love with the girl in Chicago, and she had loved me back. I had been her Ulysses. I'd been in Chicago, during the winter. The vibrant girl Chicago seems to be in the summertime is a lure, bait, because if you live in Chicago, sooner or later winter and reality are going to set in.

No one knows what it's like to be marooned in space, but I suspect it's like going through a Chicago winter with nothing but the Magikist lips and the memories of the dead for company. Uncle Herman was dead. Spokie was dead. The little girl was dead. Even the man who married the actress was dead. And the only reason I wasn't dead was because I had been lucky.

It was in Chicago that I realized I would die one day myself. It came to me on a cruel winter evening, while trundling along Stony Island in a rusted car that I wished was new, with nothing but a bag of warm goods from Harold the Fried Chicken King and the memory of what was supposed to be heaven to give me sustenance and company. This was where I learned there was no such thing as heaven. Not in the state of Illinois. It made me wonder who told rhymes to children and why they had stopped so suddenly.

D.C. Stands for Damn Confusion

I've never seen such a collection of black, brown, tan, beige, yellow, color-struck, bourgeois, bamafied, blue-veined, purple-gummed, big-legged, prim, high-minded, lowdown, hatchet-headed, half-stepping, geeked, emotional, unfeeling, go-their-own-way, fake, committed, intellectual, artistic, hopelessly ineffectual, monumentally gifted, eclectic, poetic, insufferable, irresistible, provincial, nationalistic, apologetic, loud, slow, hard, dirty, quiet and clean Negroes in my life as I have seen moving in confusing circles in and around Washington, D.C., all on U Street alone. This explains why I eventually moved nearby to them. I thrive in such confusion. It makes me feel at home.

If you're going to try to deal rationally with D.C., you have to understand it is actually supposed to be in North Carolina. Or Delaware. But in confusion it ended up between Virginia and Maryland. Benjamin Banneker and that Pierre L'Enfant fellow set the tone for the place with the plans for the city proper. What a grid it turned out to be. No spy could get out of town without first getting lost and asking directions. The place is set up like a fingerprint, and there is not another one like it in the world. Circles and hooks and wraparounds, blind leads and streets which started out as streets but became only rumors as they jumped across the Anacostia, around national monuments and under circles.

Apparently, Banneker was a genius, or he didn't care much for the time schedules of North Carolinians.

My stepfather was from North Carolina, but you couldn't have blasted him out of D.C. with dynamite. He only left once, and that was to steal my mother from Tennessee. She didn't seem to mind, either. So I had to accept that.

Everybody Else was not so understanding. Else was one of the blue-vein crowd, only he doesn't have the requisite veins. He just had an application for membership. I think he was on the waiting list. He already thought of himself as blue-veined, though, even though his application hadn't been processed, so he felt this qualified him to speak for what is called the bourgeois. My stepfather was of the purple-gum crowd, and he didn't like to be reminded of it.

But Else wouldn't forget it. Else tried to make Mother believe she had married "beneath herself," but Mother, fortunately, was middle-aged by the time she came to D.C. and knew the only thing beneath her was the ground she walked with dignity. She wasn't confused about much, certainly not about whom she had chosen to live with at this particular point. But Else would not let it rest. Else was one of those people who said black people wouldn't accept him because he was too fair and the white people wouldn't accept him because he was too dark. Else had had such a hard time. It was a wonder he still had the strength to cash his big payroll checks and chase after whatever he wanted in life. People who have had bad hard times rarely complain about having had hard times.

My stepfather, by example, had definitely had it easy,

knowing for sure he was jet black and all. People accepted him easier. He was black, all right. He was original black. So he knew where he stood. He had problems just like Everybody Else. He just had more of them.

My stepfather had wanted to be a lawyer. Fat chance of that in D.C. before '54. Now the place is crawling with black lawyers. Most of them work for things—for consortiums, for companies, for government, for think tanks, for legal firms—and not people. I cannot think of a single black lawyer in Washington, D.C., who has ever given me so much as some friendly advice. My stepfather settled for a career in the armed services and then a career in the post office. In those days, said my mother, that was the best a black man could hope for.

My stepfather was quite judicious. If he couldn't have the same aspirations and successes that white people and the blue-vein society had in Washington, D.C., he could at least know why not. He knew the government upside down and back, could talk all day about the machinations of the Supreme Court and the houses of Congress. He knew every building in D.C., and what each contained and their purposes. He suggested trips to the Library of Congress to me, gruffly. Everything he said sounded gruff. By the time I came to D.C. he was in his late forties and I was a teenager. Everybody who wasn't on the Motown or Stax labels moaning about the power of love sounded gruff to me. I was young but I figured if this black man could still be functioning with a bearing after what he had been through, then he deserved something resembling respect, even though he didn't offer much himself.

In those days I wore my hair so people would notice, long being an understatement. My stepfather saw long hair as an admission of some kind of guilt. He demanded appearances, utter cleanliness and short hair. He might not have been able to do a lot of things, but he would be clean and clipped and groomed. No one could tell him he couldn't be clean, not even the blue-veins. "Cleanliness is next to godliness," he would say, and since he had been told all his life that there weren't many ways for his blackness to come close to godliness, he took what he could get.

The man was clean. He had creases in his pants that could open letters. His chest of drawers was immaculate, everything in its place. He owned more colognes than a forest.

My stepfather tried to make me believe the only shoe to wear was a Swiss Bally, the only way to go was first class, and in order there was strength of a kind that would do well when power was unavailable and when discipline grew old. My stepfather and mother lived on Halley Place, Southeast, then on Dupont Circle in Northwest, then finally on Second Street, Southwest, before he keeled over and died one day when my mother was out. I was in St. Thomas, the Virgin Islands, changing from tan to dark brown. My stepfather was given a full military funeral and this was one of the few occurrences I've ever witnessed in D.C. which made absolute sense to me.

Now you can't blast my mother out of D.C. with dynamite and I am usually groomed. He was contagious. What goes around comes around, especially in the District. Banneker saw to it. The rest of us just carry on the great traditions.

Lem-San From Philly Invades Japan

Why Japan wasn't happening for black people in early 1987 shouldn't have been hard to figure out, especially after Prime Minister Nakasone, capturing the mood of the times, talked about how America had fallen behind in productivity and technology because black people and other dark folk were bringing down the educational system by scoring low on certain tests.

This was the message Nakasone had received from the Reagan administration, that black people were just around to lose wars. Otherwise we had to be suffered. I guess the Prime Minister's advisers were never good at breaking codes. Nakasone probably thought black people never knew anything before 1957, or whenever the American schools were integrated and abandoned and the cameras rolled and the Prime Minister got his information edited and piped overseas. He didn't know black people were around all along, or else he got the *Tarzan* script mixed up with the one from the all-time favorite movie among his learned countrymen, *Godzilla*.

This could happen because black American people didn't take loud credit for inventing fire extinguishers, fountain pens, phonographs, elevators, mail-order, shoe-lasters, lawn sprinklers, Lavalette's printing presses, clothes dryers, photographic print washers, traffic lights, Washington, D.C., certain kinds of clocks, pencil shar-peners, even the cotton gin. Yes, the cotton gin.

Oh, sure, the history books will tell you Eli Whitney invented the cotton gin. But why, pray tell, would Eli have done that? The cotton was going to be picked and cleaned and Eli was going to have little to do with that process anyway. Black people took care of that. And is not necessity the mother of invention? Then who was the lost soul who invented the cotton gin? Yet the only record is that of Eli Whitney, who owned the rights to the cotton gin. Well, all well and good for Eli Whitney and the cot-ton gin. I suppose I'll have to give him that. But what of train engine lubrication systems, sealing attachment for bottles, safety gates for bridges, mail bag transferring dev-ices, blood plasma, egg beaters, open heart surgery, port-able fire escapes, oil heaters and golf tees? I'll give you one guess.

Even I know this and I'm no scholar on these matters. This is from the top of my head and bottom of my heart. I am not the buffoon I make myself out to be, not at the time of invention. Black people know the value of modesty, if not all these inventions. Black people aren't Anglophobic about it, like Nakasone, gladly sharing the credit for inventions.

So Prime Minister Nakasone was to be excused, as long as he kept his opinions to himself. The Japanese aren't known to be particularly broad-minded anyway. Not that I know that much about it, but the Korean and Chinese peoples always seem to get an extra vein in their heads when up against the Japanese about something. In fact, I had heard the Korean was treated badly in Japan. I also had heard the Japanese have invaded mainland China once or twice before.

The way things have gone for the Chinese, no wonder

they rolled up the welcome mat on the rest of the world. The Japanese were their next-door neighbors and didn't know how to act. In fact, the way the Oriental folk carry on, you'd think they were Protestants and Catholics in Northern Ireland.

Prime Minister Nakasone was all pumped up because his people had buckled down after they lost a war and figured out how to make economical cars and cheap VCRs. I'll wager he didn't invent anything of the sort. And I wonder what Japanese-Americans thought of the Prime Minister and his sayings? They might want him to know that if he had been around in California in the early 1940s, he would have been locked up too, just like everybody else who looked like him, and it wouldn't have mattered at all how much he knew about making VCRs.

In 1988, the families of those interred were awarded twenty thousand dollars by the American government for their four years of hell. Black people wondered what ever happened to that forty acres and a mule for each family of freed slaves. That payoff never came even though it was a bargain for four hundred years of hard labor. Perhaps there was a correlation between these reparations and Japan's new place as a world economic power.

I didn't blame Nakasone any more than I blamed the Spanish-speaking café owner in Cancun, Mexico, who pulled out a rifle as four black people passed his restaurant. He was kidding, he said. He thought we'd understand. But the .22 was real. If white people had walked by the man's café and he pulled out his rifle, it would have been to offer it to them butt-first, inviting them to shoot at him to get in some target practice.

Despite my feeling that Japan was a closed society, one day in 1988 I found myself on my way there. On a plane over the Pacific, I met a darker brother. The Japanese called him Lem-san. Lem Newmius said he was from Philadelphia. This alone made him a perfect emissary to

Japan. Black people in Philadelphia are more clannish than anybody short of the Japanese. If you are black and from Philadelphia, you never really leave there. And if you do go somewhere else, you stay quiet and kick as much tail as possible in your chosen vocation before you eventually go back to where you belong.

Philadelphians usually stay in Philadelphia, figuring somehow neither they nor their city are replaceable, and rarely understood by outsiders. They can go from birth to death and in between and have no need to live anywhere else to find a place where all their dreams can come true or be utterly smashed. It's all there in Philadelphia, with the catch being you have to be Philadelphian to know how and where to find it. In Philly, black people are part of the process of life and society. White Philadelphians feel much the same as they do; however, white Philadelphians have yet to have a bomb dropped on them, as the eccentric black group called MOVE once suffered in Philly.

Black Philadelphians got over this heinous act in time. Indeed the mayor in office when this happened was a black man, and he was reelected. It seems Philly is Philly no matter what. It is home.

Lem Newmius was a son of Philadelphia, and a pioneer of sorts. He had recently moved into a magnificent house in Voorhees, New Jersey, a distance of less than a hundred miles from Philadelphia. This was quite open-minded of a black person from Philly. He was going to Japan at the behest of the Japanese. Apparently he went there often. Lem was a genius. I didn't say that first. The officers of the Hitachi Corporation did. The Japanese had gotten the idea of a nonchemical process for reproducing images. They had gotten the notion from Kodak. Kodak had never quite figured it out, so they handed it to the Japanese—for a fee, of course—and told them to see what they could do with it. The Japanese are very good at taking someone else's creative idea and putting it into production. And taking pictures without a camera was not a bad idea. This digital imaging reproduction system obviously was a great leap forward. But somebody had to figure it out in hard, applicable terms.

Lem-san was a thoughtful sort, in hard, applicable terms. When I was speaking to him, he said up front that he had no degrees from prestigious universities. I told him this had nothing to do with anything, except who would get cushy jobs with corporations. Genius was genius and if it lived, sooner or later it would manifest itself. Lem-san smiled at me. He said he was just a tinkerer. His father had been a tinkerer, always taking things apart and putting them back together just to see how they worked. Lem-san said he could only give credit for his genius to God and his father, and, of course, Philly. I told him this was as it should be.

Imagine if you will no need for film processing, for pictures which could be recorded on computer disks and stored by the millions in less than a square foot, and transmitted instantly at any time. And not just those carnival scan reproductions of the kind which can be put on T-shirts.

That's how far the Japanese had gotten on the idea when they ran across Lem-san, who was working for a small U.S. company which specialized in photo identification cards. What the Japanese needed were high-quality, high-resolution photos, like those in *Life* magazine. So the Japanese wrote their computations on a blackboard. Lem had looked at the computations and said politely, "Well, that's close, but if we do this . . . and this . . . and this . . ." As Lem spoke, he erased the computations and wrote in his own. And the men representing the Hitachi Corporation had nodded and said, "Ah . . . Ah . . . Ah . . ." They immediately saw how far Lem-san could take them.

Nakasone would be pleased with not just reproductions, but full-color, high-resolution images, formed digitally. I told Lem-san I hoped he'd get some credit as I left him in the clutches of the smiling men from the Hitachi Corporation at Narita Airport outside Tokyo.

I laughed to myself for the remainder of the short time I stayed in Japan, even though nothing funny happened while I was there. A Japanese man steered me through his language and assisted me because we worked for the same large corporation. He had an assistant who was Korean. He informed me that this Korean assistant was not to be trusted and might steal things if not watched closely. The Korean man dropped his head. I had seen all this before, of course.

Then I saw thin black mannequins in the store window, all with caricatured features. I walked down the Ginza alone, performed my functions and left. Soon after this, the Japanese relieved Nakasone of his duties as Prime Minister and replaced him with someone who was better at public relations. I wondered if Nakasone would visit Philadelphia while in his retirement. Probably not. Me, I go often.

About Life

Where Are the Black Men?

From time to time some concerned person or magazine article will ask the question: Where are the black men? Usually the people most interested in the answer are black women, which probably means they're the only ones who care. Usually the question is asked in one form or another by *Essence* magazine, every November, like clockwork.

This question compels me since I am usually near a mirror when I am asked: Where are the black men? I decided to resolve this, lest I become schizophrenic, whatever that is. Black men can't afford to be seen with schizophrenia. If a black man is judged schizophrenic, then he must have stolen it from somebody. So he is sent to the penitentiary.

Of course! The penitentiary! There are many black men in penitentiaries. Some of them probably even deserve to be there. The black slab of granite! There are black men on this Vietnam Memorial and the Revolutionary War Memorial in Washington, D.C. You may argue that these are not men, just names. But when you are looking for black men, you take what you can get. I see a few black men in movies about the Vietnam War. Since white men usually write the scripts for these movies, the black actors usually portray incoherent fools. I guess that's how they wound up in granite.

Many black men are in the same places poor white, yellow and red men are. Nobody has ever told these men that they ought to be in pictures, unless their names were Li'l Abner, Chan or Tonto. Take the picture of the completion of the transcontinental railroad. Chinese men built that railroad under duress. In a late nineteenth-century photo of the recently finished transcontinental railroad at Promontory Point, Utah, there are plenty of proud men standing around, but not a yellow one is in sight. So where are the black men? Maybe some of them are with the yellow men on the other side of the railroad tracks, taking out their frustrations on each other. There is nothing like a missed photo opportunity to bring out the worst in people.

Sometimes you can come closer to the location of black men by figuring out where they aren't. For sure, they aren't in the White House or the Senate. What's left? The mayor's office! Eureka! Quite a few black men are at any mayors' conference. I hate to say I told you so, but if you follow the process of elimination, it's easy to find the black men.

Since we're speaking of the process of elimination, if you were in South Africa, the question of where are the black men would be a real poser, even though ten or twenty or thirty million or so black men—who really knows for sure?--are there. But you would need a miner's helmet and some real intestinal fortitude to find most of them. If you work for a foreign service newspaper, radio or television network, you can hardly find any black men in South Africa at all, and if you should get lucky and run across a couple of unentombed ones, you can't even tell anybody you saw them, unless they have been given a governmental stamp of approval beforehand. How's that for luck? That's what apartheid means: Where are the black men, and how long can we keep them there?

In places like south-central Los Angeles and depressed

areas in Detroit and Chicago, there are platoons of young black men who are in gangs with names like the Crips and the Bloods. Their names are not on any black slab of granite. Not yet. They like carrying around heavy weaponry like Uzi machine guns, assault rifles, 9-mm pistols and pump-action shotguns and the like. Then they wait until another young man makes what they consider a wrong move and they blast away. They have seen from history, and from Rambo, that if you are cool, this is the thing to do. Blow away the uncool.

So they smoke cocaine and sell it—where they get this cocaine is anybody's guess, since these boys are nobody's horticulturalists—and ride around with their brains scoured out and think that everybody is making uncool moves and they blast away. They like to blast away for gold rope chains and they consider buying a Mercedes-Benz life goal number one. They reach this at age eighteen or so, and having nowhere else to go, decide to commit suicide by committing murder. There is no sense pressing these young black men with logic. They see no logic in their poverty. They see the only acceptance they've ever known while in a mob. And these are the young black men who wind up in the movies.

If young white men are shown in a group activity in a movie, it's *Chariots of Fire,* a movie about noble white sprinters, or *Hoosiers,* a movie about noble white basketball players. If young black men are shown in a group activity, it's *Colors,* a movie about psychopathic behavior. I could have sworn I've seen a noble black sprinter or basketball player or two. But who am I going to believe, the movies or my own eyes? Movies help convince these young black men they are on a proper course. But I would like to inform the lot of them, I know where all the gold and diamonds in the world are located. South Africa. If these young men want to be cool, down, or whatever it's called now, they need to go take an entire gold mine. Of course, the "owners" of these gold mines are not going to take this lying down. The present proprietors are going to shoot first and ask questions later, but I'm sure this will be no problem to the Crips and Bloods. According to their public relations department, they are the toughest things going and fear nothing, not even death. So they should go to South Africa. It would make a ripsnorting movie.

After the location shoot, the Crips and Bloods can trade the gold and diamonds to the Germans for all the Mercedes-Benzes that can be put on several large boats. The Germans, being German, would be more than happy to trade in this manner, I'd guess. While the Crips and Bloods are at it, they can arrange to have Nelson Mandela released from the penitentiary. Then I'd be willing to bet nobody would be asking where the black men are. They would be at the polls in a democratic South Africa, encouraged to go by the spirit of Mandela, where they would summarily vote the Crips and Bloods and any remaining generals out of office.

Then the Crips and Bloods could drive luxuriously to some other conflict. Writers would make up things about them. There would be photo opportunities. It would give people something worthwhile to tell their grandchildren. But until such a day, I admit the validity of the question about the whereabouts of black men. I'm also smug because I know where some are. I have the phone numbers. Sometimes I call a black man and ask, "Where are the black men?" The black man on the other end unfailingly replies, "I'm on the phone with you, Dumbo, when I could be doing something productive. I'm just beneath the surface. S'matter, you blind?" This always makes me feel better even though I've just been insulted.

As far as insults go, I've heard worse.

On the Natural Superiority of Black Athletes

Are black people, all people of African descent but especially African-American men, naturally superior athletes? If you are asking me, I'd have to say, not that I've noticed. But why ask in the first place? I want to know why black men have to be naturally superior athletes. If we are, it would inevitably follow that black men are naturally inferior at something else. Like thinking. Trust me. If not me, trust history. Go back to Germany fifty years ago. Go back a hundred years, to the Trail of Tears toward Oklahoma. Go to South Africa next weekend. It follows. It follows black people are not quite . . . right. Not quite . . . human.

So the question becomes why ask? Ego? Sour grapes? More? This is no choice and I'd rather not see it reach that point, so I will attempt to shatter the theory of racial athletic superiority with an expert exhibition of word processor boxing. I'm going to set you up, then hit you with the clincher.

First, some particulars:

Jimmy "the Greek" Snyder was at Duke Zeibert's restaurant in Georgetown in January 1988, just as Doug

Williams was about to play quarterback for the Washington Redskins in the Super Bowl. Snyder intimated that black people were better athletes because they had been bred to be that way, with large thighs which shot up into their backs.

On a "Nightline" interview from Houston in the spring of 1987, Al Campanis, an executive with the Los Angeles Dodgers, said he believed black people lacked "the necessities" to be field or general managers. "How many are good swimmers?" he asked. "Or pitchers?" Somewhere, three men named Frank Robinson, Anthony Nesty and Dwight Gooden weren't laughing. Here was institutional racism in the flesh, in all its suicidal, self-aggrandizing debasement.

Early in 1989, Tom Brokaw hosted an NBC program entitled "The Black Athlete: Fact and Fiction," then went on to utterly ignore the facts for the speculations of two scientists. Present in panel form were Dr. Harry Edwards, the Berkeley sociologist; Arthur Ashe, the author and former tennis champion; two scientists who were not named Mengele. Others, like baseball star Mike Schmidt and Olympian Carl Lewis, were heard from on videotape. This program accomplished one feat—it flushed out a certain . . .

Roger Stanton, publisher of pulp sports magazines, who wrote Brokaw a letter. And it was not a love letter. Stanton: ". . . black players lack discipline, and they are the ones most likely to get into trouble . . . [A] black player in general pays less attention to such things as showing up on time or following a rigid routine . . . [Edwards's] contention that blacks turn to athletics because they cannot do well in other professions is ridiculous. They can be lawyers, doctors or businessmen if they so desire. But it takes hard work and discipline, and in many instances they are not willing to pay the price . . . Quarterback is a very intricate position and there are not many blacks qualified . . . if you gave twenty white college football players an IQ test, the whites would outshine the blacks every time."

We can strike Snyder and Campanis. You could nearly understand them. They were old, fat with the kill, and drunk or getting there. Television cameras and reporters Ed Hotaling and Ted Koppel happened to show up at the wrong time for them. Stanton was ignorant, which would be fine, except he had the forum to disseminate his ignorance. He undoubtedly kowtowed to journalism's double standard regarding black and white athletes. A middle-aged black former athlete "overdoses on drugs," and his immoral carcass is laid open on journalism's streets. A middle-aged white former athlete "has a heart attack of undetermined cause" and we are told how much he loved children. Stanton also wrote that Doug Williams's brilliant performance in the 1988 Super bowl "may have been a fluke." Stanton is inaccurate here. Make that four flukes. In one quarter. On one leg.

But why would a sober sort like Brokaw enter this debacle? His program, while it attempted seriousness, played like badly tuned farce. Here the doctors were advancing the fast-twitch, slow-twitch muscle theory which states that black people from a certain region of Africa (they can't make up their minds if it is East or West Africa) and their more immediate descendants are better at explosive sports, sprints in track, short distances, hoop, while Europeans have slow-twitch muscles which enable them to win the longer races. This came after an Olympics where white men had won the gold medals in basketball and volleyball, which are quite explosive sports.

Meanwhile, blacks from Kenya dominated the long-distance races out on the track, and later Ethiopians dominated the Boston Marathon and world cross-country championships. The Russian Valery Borzov, a white man, won the Olympic gold medal in hundred meters in 1972. The Russians won the four-by-hundred-meter relay in

1988 as well. And the world two-hundred-meter record holder is not Carl Lewis, but an Italian, of all people, Pietro Mennea. No one on Tom Brokaw's special brought this up, least of all the doctors, who were too busy admitting they were testing the muscle fibers in all these cute little children's legs.

It was weird.

Then came the tape of Mike Schmidt, saying he would have to agree that black men seem to have the edge as natural athletes. I guess they never had any mirrors in the clubhouse of the Philadelphia Phillies, for whom Schmidt toiled so long and so well. Mike Schmidt is only the greatest third baseman in the history of major league baseball. Lots of black men have played third base in the major leagues since Jackie Robinson broke the color line. Yet Schmidt still thinks black men are naturally superior athletes. He'd always wanted to slam-dunk, but he could only hit 548 home runs in the Show. Poor Schmitty.

Then came Carl Lewis, who said black athletes seemed to be "made better." Carl can be narcissistic. If he was Serbo-Croatian, they would be "made better," no doubt. Ashe said, "My head tells me yes, but my heart tells me no," or vice versa, on the question. The greatest victory of Ashe's career came at Wimbledon in 1975, when he defeated Jimmy Connors. By this time, Connors, who is white, was quicker and hit harder than Ashe. Connors was, in fact, the number one player in the world. But Ashe outthought him, refusing to play power against power. Ashe moved the ball around, gave Connors nothing to feed off, and won on guile as much as athletic ability. But his heart said no and his head said yes, or vice versa. Ashe had recently completed a compendium entitled *The History of the Black Athlete,* so I assume he was caught up in his subject matter.

Many older black people subscribe to the theory that black men are naturally superior athletes. No way you can convince them otherwise. There are reasons for their attitude. Before the integration of sports in this country (which came after the aberration of Jack Johnson, and began in the boxing ring with Joe Louis and in baseball with Jackie Robinson), all the testimonials were that black people were naturally *inferior* athletically, as in everything else. Black men could not develop the mental discipline it took to go fifteen rounds, or play second base in a taut, 2–1 World Series game.

Blacks wouldn't work hard enough. Athletics had a mental side then, and a work-ethic side. Mentally, ethically, black men could accomplish nothing without a white man behind them with a whip. That was what was publicized, and thus became the apparent consensus.

Then along came Joe Louis, knocking out the apparent consensus, represented by Max Schmeling, a strong boxer who through no fault of his own happened to be employed by one Adolf Hitler. So even many white people got behind Joe. But all along white people had Tarzan, the Green Hornet, Superman, Batman, movie stars, presidents, publicized aviators and captains of industry. Having escaped the shackles of slavery a bare seventy-five years, black people had *Birth of a Nation* and "Amos 'n' Andy" as the total of publicized cultural reparations. Financial reparations were not forthcoming. In this kind of hostile environment, as you might imagine, Joe Louis became Tarzan, the Green Hornet, Superman, Batman, movie stars, etc., all rolled into one. Joe dared not lose. Lose, in the one place where the field was almost level? Out of the question.

Recently I was a victim on "Tony Brown's Journal," where a debate was raised on this thorny issue. I explained that in boxing, for example, the fighters had come from poor backgrounds. Fighting was their last resort. That's why they were good at it. After the taping, a well-dressed middle-aged black man came up to me and said, "Michael Jordan's parents weren't poor. So how do you explain Michael Jordan?"

I laughed and told the man that I really couldn't blame

anybody for watching Michael Jordan play basketball and thinking he was not quite human. But then I said, "Did you know he was once cut from his high school basketball team?" And then I said, "You know, just because Air Jordan is the best basketball player on earth, that is no reflection on you. All the credit goes to Mikey, hard work and God."

From Barbara Turpin, Ph.D., assistant professor of psychology at Southwest Missouri State University: "There is a sociological side to the belief that genetics is the sole cause of black athletic superiority and white intellectual ability. Whites can say, "Well, of course I'm not like Isiah Thomas; I don't have the genes," or blacks can say (and I've heard my black students say it), "Well, of course I can't get a doctorate; I don't have the genes for it." It allows people to avoid taking responsibility for their own behaviors. And a genetic determination argument allows racism to have a scientific basis, and justifies the denial of opportunity to the 'inferior' group."

Dr. Alvin Poussaint, psychiatrist, consultant to "The Cosby Show," among others, describes it as a "dangerous theory." He says, "In some whites there is an unwillingness to face the fact that black athletes work harder. . . . Throughout the years of discrimination, blacks began to see sport as survival. You do what you've been trained to do. But along the way, the traits which made [them] able to excel at sports—mental acuity, mental concentration, mental toughness, work ethic—the very traits which blacks weren't supposed to have and supposedly were the reason to keep them out of sports in the first place, now those traits are given little or no credence. Why don't we look at the mental work within the sport? . . . If the attitude of the majority and minority was more open, more blacks would become mathematicians and scientists. Right now, it's a matter of a self-fulfilling prophecy."

To those black students who don't think they have the

genes for doctorates, know that black people invented a few things, even without a Batman to inspire them. When you talk about the real McCoy, you are not talking about Walter Brennan, but about Elijah McCoy, who was an inventor of train engine lubrication systems, not a Green Bay Packer running back.

So here is the most immediately negative ramification of the black athlete theory. It stunts and denudes black men, who are the largest virtually untapped natural resource left in this country, a a time when it needs its resources.

Once I had a conversation with Howie Long, the All-Pro defensive lineman of the L.A. Raiders. Long, who is white, was raving over John Elway, the All-Pro quarterback of the Denver Broncos. John Elway is white, too. After saying how great Elway was, Long told me, "You know, Ralph, he plays like a brother." I raised my eyebrows. Howie said, "Here comes that brother shit." I gently reminded him he brought up brothers, I hadn't. Howie paused, then looked as though somebody had hit him in the face with an ax handle.

A white former colleague of mine likes to point out the Chinese consider themselves athletically inferior to whites and far inferior to blacks. Well, not all Chinese. The world high-jump record holder at seven-foot-ten was a tall man from China. Did he Zen his way over the bar, or what? The greatest female track athlete I ever saw was Chi Chen, also Chinese. For flexibility and versatility, Chen made Florence Griffith-Joyner look like, well, a girl. Michael Chang, the seventeen-year-old second generation Chinese-American, did not win the 1989 French Open because the epicanthic folds of his eyes helped him see the ball better, did he?

The games belong to the people who play them well.

Some of these players were white men like Bill Walton, Valery Brumel, Jerry West, John Havlicek, Tom Chambers, Mark McGwire, George Case, Rex Chapman,

Terry Bradshaw, Joe Montana, Dick Butkus, Max Baer, Pete Maravich, Hugh McElhenny, Paul Westphal, Dave Cowens, Bob Lilly, Bruce Jenner, Will Clark, Bobby Jones, Bob Mathias, Roger Staubach, Billy Cunningham, Don Hutson, Glenn Davis, Babe Ruth, Ted Wiliams, Ty Cobb, Mickey Mantle, Cal Ripken, Jr., Boris Becker, Sergei Bubka, Lance Alworth . . . say, this is getting boring, isn't it?

You might say some of these not-quite-human athletes are no longer playing. What has that to do with it? Did all white people stop being able to play once a few retired? Or did attitudes change when America noticed most athletic heroes were black?

Boxing is the clincher. It is the purest form of sport, one man trying to stop another, and defending himself. It is not for the faint of heart or the satisfied. In the early part of this century, there were great Irish boxers, great Jewish boxers, great Italian boxers, but hardly any of those exist anymore because they have found in assimilation work and in many cases good fortune. Work and good fortune are more reliable than boxing. Now, and most assuredly all along, there have been great black boxers. Does this mean blacks are naturally superior boxers, because they still do it? Only if you're not paying attention.

By way of example, I offer the June 12, 1989, fight to a draw between Sugar Ray Leonard and Thomas "Hit Man" Hearns.

In my opinion, Leonard and Hearns are two of the greatest prizefighters of this era. They are in their early thirties now, so a lot of talk was going around that they shouldn't be fighting. They were washed up. Well of course they shouldn't have been fighting, but where else could two black men earn twenty-four million dollars in one night? On June 12, they fought back and forth, taking turns hurting each other with brilliant exhibitions of the science, for twelve brutal rounds. There is a young boxer named Michael Nunn—black, of course—who is in the same weight class as Leonard and Hearns. Much is made of what he will do to them one day. And I have no doubt he shall. But if he had been in that ring on June 12, against either Hearns or Leonard, Nunn would have been knocked out, because these two champion boxers went beyond mere athletic skill.

Hearns knocked Leonard down in the third round, beating him to the draw as they both threw rights. Leonard had decided to go for Hearns early with a lightning right lead. But Hearns was up to the mark for it and threw his at the same time and it was a question of landing most correctly, in the most debilitating fashion. It was a question of inches, and for that split second, Hearns was a better problem-solver. Leonard went down a few missed punches later after that right caught him flush on the button of his chin. Leonard got up. He came back and hurt Hearns with a three-punch combination in the fifth. Hearns wobbled around the ring, tying Leonard up to survive. Leonard pinned him on the ropes, looking for the clincher. But Hearns threw a sharp left hook to Leonard's body, which made Ray reconsider. Hearns made it to the end of the round and stumbled back to his corner.

Emanuel Steward, Hearns's trainer-manager and another black man, kneeled in front of Hearns as he sat on the stool in the corner. Steward did not yell, or try to tell Hearns what he had done wrong. Steward said, "This is what makes a great fighter. This is what's going to make you great. Do you understand me, Tommy?" Hearns shook away the fog and nodded. He understood. There was nothing Steward could tell Hearns about boxing—Hearns is the world champion, not Steward.

But Steward could tell Hearns about life, about what it takes to live it well, to survive. To do this, he would have to come back from being hurt. I can guarantee you, the average middle-class black or white would have at this point said, "Well, that's enough of that," and asked

Steward to cut his gloves off. Because to the average middle-class man, this would be the way to survive.

Hearns went out and hurt Leonard some more. In the seventh round, a quick left hook off the jab, a punch Hearns wasn't supposed to have, took Sugar Ray by surprise and only Ray's keen, learned talent for slipping punches took him through to the end of the round. Leonard was the best boxer alive at the time. Now he drew from within himself, his past. He went back and hurt Hearns and continued hurting him until the eleventh round. Hearns had been using his left, and had gotten Ray's attention. Hearns hardly threw the right. Ray hurt Hearns badly at the end of the ninth round, and in the tenth. But while hurting Hearns, he was disregarding the man's right more and more. Between the tenth and eleventh rounds, Steward told the truth in a boxing sense. "Throw your right hand, Tommy!" he beseeched. "They're begging you to throw the right hand! The right hand will take you home, Tommy!"

Leonard came into the eleventh looking for a knockout. A sleepy-looking Hearns casually measured him with the outstretched left jab. Briefly, Leonard may have considered the left hook Hearns had used in the fifth and seventh rounds. He never saw the right. I videotaped this and ran the sequence back frame by frame. In one frame, Hearns's right was cocked, his left measuring Leonard. In the next frame, Hearns has already followed through with the right. It has already landed, and Leonard has been hurt. If that's washed up, I'm the Duke of Windsor. Leonard, hurt badly, was down a few punches later. But by sheer will, by mental capacity alone, he rose up, and by the end of the round was back in Hearns's chest, firing with both hands.

Leonard won the twelfth round going away. They refused to buckle, wilt, die. The will they displayed was palpable. At ringside, a white man, Jim Lampley, a broadcaster for HBO, said, "You will seldom see a greater display of what it is that makes men fighters." His colleague, Larry Merchant, said, "This had nothing to do with [boxing]; this had to do with what these two men are made of." And if Jim Lampley and Larry Merchant never say another mouthful, they did then.

Later, after I left Las Vegas, I was riding in a rough part of East Oakland, California, with a friend. We passed a corner where three or four young boys were standing. One of the boys was eleven or twelve, and he had decided to pick on another boy, who seemed to be about nine. They were both thin, poorly dressed, unkempt and of African descent. The bigger boy ran around the smaller boy and wrapped him in a bear hug. Then he quickly punched the smaller boy in the head with a right. Hard. Not like television. Real. The older boy performed his coward's trick again, and again. After the third hard right to the head, the smaller boy bounced away from the bigger boy, enraged. He pumped his fist almost happily. The older boy looked at him and something changed in his eyes. And then my friend, who was driving, turned the corner. Now some people might say, "Well, you two are grown men. Why didn't you stop them?" Those are the same people who might ask if black men are naturally superior athletes. "So now the little kid won't have to fight again tomorrow," I said to my sober friend, who nodded knowingly. He is also a black man who has a son. "Either that or he'll have very tough skin by the time he's eighteen," he said. I nodded back.

Now if this is what you want to call the natural athletic superiority of the black male athlete, then so be it for you. Some of us call it survival, though.

Them rights hurt.

Witness for the Prosecution

On October 12, 1989, Ralph David Abernathy, Martin Luther King's former friend turned sycophant and steadfast witness to the sixties' civil rights movement, came again to Memphis beneath a storm of protest. This time it was Abernathy who had the dream. If Martin Luther King turned over in his grave, J. Edgar Hoover was quite blissful in his.

Under the aegis of Harper & Row publishers in New York, Abernathy had written an autobiography entitled *And the Walls Came Tumbling Down.* When Abernathy endorsed Ronald Reagan for President in 1980, there was but a lifted eyebrow of surprise. When he went to the twentieth anniversary of the March on Washington, he wasn't listed in the program. His two strokes were footnotes as far as the mass media had been concerned. He had been a mere backdrop to history. Yet David, as he and his family and even King himself have always called Abernathy, said he knew something the rest of us didn't know because he had been there.

His book refers to Dr. King's alleged visit to two women the night before his assassination on April 4, 1968, and a fight between King and another woman, a visitor from Nashville, in his room at the Lorraine Motel in the early hours of the morning. This was publicized in such a risqué manner it seemed only as an old footnote that King was later shot in the neck with a rifle.

The outrage was quick, righteous, plain. A letter of repudiation was drafted and signed by twenty-seven black leaders in Atlanta. Jesse Jackson, Andy Young and all King's men said their remembrances differed sharply from David's. David slowly said, "I have been honest and truthful." All this is known among the streetwise young people and wizened publishers as "juice." Juice, i.e. publicity, sells books. Hadn't John F. Kennedy and Hoover had their names linked with sexual athletics? But neither of those men had a national holiday named for him. No one whose life was changed for the better by King necessarily wanted to know if he was *that* human. But in book publishing, that is the way it goes. Books have a difficult time attracting attention on their own merits. Books emit neither light nor sound unless they are read, and sometimes, usually, not even then. Books need juice . . .

The occasion was the Memphis Book and Author dinner, held at the Peabody Hotel. Five authors were called to flog their books. Abernathy entered balancing on his wife, Juanita, who had the look of a deer under headlights. I was present, as was one of my friends from high school who was now a detective downtown. We had been in the tenth grade and a few miles away when King was killed. He informed me that the two stern black men who flanked Mr. and Mrs. Abernathy were police sharpshooters, former SWAT team members. If only King had been given such sharpshooters in his defense. But they didn't exist then, not officially. Largely due to King's life, the sharpshooters enjoyed their current station. David's eyes held fast to a dreamy look.

The authors spoke. Ruth Coe Chambers talked about pierced ears. Madison Smartt Bell talked about judging people as individuals and nascent racism and nearly cried.

(He is white.) Paul Hemphill read about his father and a truck named Dixie Red Ball and chafed in proximity to Bell. I told a hoary joke about two writers. They see two silver quarters in a commode. One writer throws in five dollars. The other asks why. The first writer says, "You didn't think I was going to reach in there for fifty cents, did you?" I told that one for David's sake. Everyone else laughed.

Abernathy spoke last, in a painfully slow manner. His hands looked like wax as he slid them up the lectern. It would be difficult for a man so weakened to compose a book, especially a man who said, "Hosea Williams do not know what happened," without intending dialect. Daniel Bial is the senior editor at Harper & Row who handled Abernathy's book. Normally ghostwriters are on the covers of as-told-to books. In this case, they would become lightning rods for outrage. How many ghostwriters worked? "None," said Bial.

Abernathy told how the Reverend Vernon Johns, a forerunner for the movement, had referred to his constituency—to himself—as "Nigras." He also said Johns was "John the Baptist," obviously the forerunner to a Christ-like King. Someone in the audience softly asked, "Then who is Judas?" Abernathy talked of Atlanta being "the capital of the world," and said it was a place "where I might not be welcome anymore." He'd helped black people go from the back of the bus to the front. "Now," he said, "it's time to own the bus."

Undoubtedly his book sold better than if he had merely said Martin Luther King, Jr., slept here. But David failed to recall that bottom-line economics is one reason for racism. Racism can be a racket just like nearly everything else. "I grew up one of twelve children in a six-room house in the Black Belt of Alabama," he said. "We had a fireplace in every room. Every winter morning, my father woke me before dawn to start fires in each fireplace. Well,

I'm tired of starting fires." He left Memphis the next day, Friday the thirteenth of October, as the sky over the endless delta dawned blue and new children were being born and nothing really changed.

What Annoys Black People Most

The question "What annoys You People most?" was first brought to my attention by an educated, well-meaning white person at a cocktail party where I was one of the few black people available for study. I knew the person who asked me this was well-meaning because the question was vastly less annoying than "What do You People want?" "What do You People want?" means "What are You People doing at this cocktail party, ruining my one chance to get shitfaced and hog the conversation?" Compared to that, "What annoys You People most?" was a *bon mot* almost as felicitous and welcome as "Hello."

And so, instead of merely excusing myself, my response was "Well, if We People really want to know, get me a good car, some research materials and three years' worth of expenses and I will come back in three years and reveal my findings." This offer was of course rejected in the blink of an eye, so I was reduced to educated, well-meaning guesswork.

I went out one day for lunch determined to find things which worked on my nerves. I drove in lunch-hour traffic in a major metropolitan city in the East. Washington, if you must know. Any number of my fellow drivers annoyed me straightaway just by being there. And then there was a woman driving a Volkswagen Rabbit. She rode my bumper so close that one service station mechanic we passed waved us into his garage for repairs. He believed I was towing her. I nonchalantly looked in the rearview mirror and there she was hitting me with her high beams and calling me everything but Rudolph the Red-Nosed Reindeer.

So I moved over to the right to let her by. She raced ahead, pulled over in front of me, then slowed down. Soon we stopped at a red light. She was doing her hair when the light turned green. Then she proceeded to do her nails. I sat there, quite annoyed. If she had not been a very pretty woman, I likely would have gone past annoyed and moved directly to upset. Suddenly, a tractor trailer blew its horn in my ear. Then a bus lurched out in front of me. Then a cabdriver gave me the finger. Then a police car followed me for twelve blocks. These occurrences didn't annoy me. I am accustomed to them.

I arrived at my destination, the Mid-City Fish Market at Fourteenth and P streets. The Mid-City Fish Market is an establishment operated by Korean immigrants and their children and other relatives, and patronized by a United Nations of clientele (minus diplomatic apparel and limousines), including at this particular time a West Indian, a Saudi, an Irishman, a Jewish couple and a full complement of You People, all of whom seemed to appreciate the hot fish dinners, if nothing else. None of this bothered me in the slightest.

I went outside. Sitting there gleaming on this inner-city street was a beautiful brand-new van, painted a forest green. A name of a brand of cigarettes was emblazoned on the van, which carried two occupants in its cab, a Latino man and a black woman. Both of them were from New York. They were handing out complimentary packs of this particular cigarette, which I call Green Death.

If you start smoking this brand of cigarette, none other

can satisfy your craving, and since most other cigarettes contain nicotine, this is surely curious. What was it about Green Death that was so irreplaceable once your lungs got used to it? *I didn't know.* That annoyed me, not knowing. Actually, the not knowing annoyed me greatly, because I too inhale Green Death at regular intervals. I felt stupid. Feeling stupid annoys me.

After having traversed life's minefield of semi-mandatory stays at the penitentiaries, hard drugs, crooks, police, scientific experimentation, falling masonry, New York City, Detroit, after having avoided being hit by buses or trains, being lucky enough never to fly in the wrong airplane, or through any rice paddies, after all this dumb, blind luck, I ended up being done in by the toxicity of the Green Death, by my own weak hand. And I knew it. I caved in to it. Being weak is extremely tiresome.

The motto of the Green Death was "Alive With Pleasure!" or some such insult. This motto was painted on the van. I hid my annoyance—I am adept at this—and struck up a conversation with the van's two smiling occupants.

"Nice van," I said.

"Yep," he said.

"You get paid to ride in this sweet van up and down the coast and give out free cigarettes?" I asked.

"Get paid good money, too. It's not what you know," she said. "It's who you know. We're bringing this so all y'all will catch cancer. Ha, ha, ha. Great, isn't it?"

"I'll say it is," I said heartily.

I went on to a television taping session, where I was to take part in a panel discussion on forgettable issues. I was not paid for being on this panel, but that caused me only minor chafing. I am not greedy. Sometimes it annoys me because I haven't sunk to that level yet.

There was a man on the panel who pestered me greatly, though. I am always annoyed by people who talk in a nonracist way but don't act in a nonracist manner.

This man talked like a Quaker but had the disposition of a crocodile. Dishonesty is bothersome. But this is only a mild annoyance, one easily lost by parting company. And there is no quicker way to part company with me than with lame ethnic humor. Nothing irks me quite in the same manner as lame ethnic humor. It's like being locked in the same room with a sick stranger suffering from and unleashing severe gas pains.

Once a white man and I had an appointment. Suits were appropriate, so we both wore one. I wore a plain black suit, flat, no frills. In a trademark example of lame ethnic humor, this man said to me, "So where are all your girls?" If I put on a suit that fits, I have to hear a pimp joke. He couldn't say, "The suit looks good on you." That would have been too easy. Yet I couldn't blame him. He was from the same racist structure as I was and he had always acted in a nonracist manner around me. So I didn't issue one of my standard salvos for such pitiful jokes, which would have been something like "Where are all my girls? Over at your mother's house, getting ready." It annoys me when I'm immature—but only if I can't get a good line out of it.

As for other things that annoy black people most, I could only offer a short list of further guesswork based on my own experiences, and that would not be fair to the rest of You People. There are days when everything pesters me, so I am not a good example. But by casually asking around, I have found out toothpaste dried in the basin annoys some black people. Others don't care for a fly in the house. Others will take the fly, as long as they don't have to put up with in-laws. Some black people hate for someone to stick the peanut butter knife into the jelly jar without wiping it off first. But some don't even mind that. The space program annoys black people who live in Chicago and have never even been downtown. Any mention of the name Al Sharpton annoys some black New Yorkers. Others would swear by him. An old photograph of a lynching seems to gather unanimous antipathy among You People. Even more annoying are people who say, "Yes, terrible, but that could never happen here."

Insecure white people annoy black people, and the general suspicion is that this annoying is done on purpose. It annoys black people to realize they still have only the vaguest idea of what the purpose for this annoying could be. Reasons, sure. Greed, ignorance, fear, boredom, all good reasons to annoy people, but what of purpose? Finding no purpose in life is the apex of annoyance, so finally, there is a small but hardy group of black people who have thrown up their hands and to whom everything is an annoyance if they can't eat it, drink it or . . . well, on second thought, perhaps I should leave them with their anonymity.

My conclusion is that generalities are unsound and annoying people with them can be dangerous. I hope this has helped to clear the air. If it hasn't, what do you expect of me? Miracles? You do? Well, so do I. This annoys me most.